A Guide
to the Bodhisattava's
Way of Life

❖

Sanskrit: Bodhisattvacharyavatara
Tibetan: Byang-chub sems-pa'i spyod-pa-la 'jug-pa

Translated
by
Stephen Batchelor

LIBRARY OF TIBETAN WORKS AND ARCHIVES

Cover Photo: H.J. Schwabl. From the collection of the mu-
seum of Library of Tibetan Works and Archives.

ISBN: 81-85102-59-7

Published by the Library of Tibetan Works and Archives,
Dharamsala, and printed at Indraprastha Press, (CBT),
New Delhi-110002.

Foreword

We are happy to be bring out this sixth reprint of this very popular work, "A Guide to the Bodhisattva's Way of Life", an English translation of "Bodhisattvacharyavatara" (Tib: *Byang-chub sems-pa'i spyod-pa-la 'jug-pa*). This great work was composed by Shantideva, an eighth century Buddhist master at the monastic university of Nalanda in northern India. Outwardly, Shantideva was a monk strictly observing the code of monastic discipline, secretly he was a realized tantric adept, but most important of all he was a Bodhisattva motivated by the awakening mind, the wish to achieve Buddhahood to be able to liberate all sentient beings likewise.

Since the first publication of this translation more than ten years ago, Shantideva's work has become much more widely known, due notably to His Holiness the Dalai Lama's efforts. He has taught and explained it often, particularly extolling the very practical nature of the advice it contains.

Ably translated into English by Stephen Batchelor, in accordance with an oral teaching by Geshe Ngawang Dhargyey on the commentary "The Ocean of Good Explanation" by Thogme Zangpo, Shantideva's "A Guide to the Bodhisattva's Way of Life" will continue to inspire readers with the higher ideals of Bodhisattvas while repeatedly encouraging their practical application in every day life.

Gyatsho Tshering
Director

March 1998

Contents

Contents

Translator's Introduction

Shantideva, a Buddhist master from the monastic university of Nalanda, India, composed his work "A Guide to the Bodhisattva's Way of Life" (*Bodhisattvacharyavatara*) in the eighth century of the Christian era. In India at that time Mahayana Buddhism was well established and in the thousand or so stanzas of this text we find a concise yet comprehensive account of the principal features of this doctrine.

In contrast with the Arhat of Hinayana Buddhism—the being who has secured his own liberation from the misery of cyclic existence—Mahayana Buddhism has as its ideal the Bodhisattva who, uninterested in his liberation alone, strives for the well being of all living creatures.

The Bodhisattva comes into being with the development of the Awakening Mind, the pure altruistic wish to achieve the state of a Buddha, and with this motivation he then proceeds to engage in a way of life that is conducive to the realisation of his goal. In the first chapter of this work we shall see how Shantideva introduces the aspirant to the Awakening Mind and inspires him to develop it; in the second, how the mind is prepared; and in the third chapter how the Bodhisattva's vow itself is finally taken. From this point onward the author continues to elucidate the means whereby to fulfil this commitment, namely through the practices of Moral Discipline (chapter 4-5), Patience (chapter 6), Enthusiasm (chapter 7), Meditation (chapter 8), and wisdom (chapter 9). In the final chapter, the merits gained from the composition of the work are dedicated to the welfare of all beings in the form of a prayer. Hence this short but significant work contains the essential points of Mahayana Buddhist practice and for over a thousand years has acted as a guide for people throughout

India, Tibet, China and Mongolia who have wished to follow this path.

In the autumn of 1974, in response to the request of several Western Buddhists studying in Dharamsala, India, His Holiness the Dalai Lama encouraged and gave his blessing to the undertaking at the Library of Tibetan Works and Archives of a project to translate Shantideva's *Bodhi- sattvacharyavatara*. In order to do this, he suggested that the "Ocean of Good Explanation", a commentary to the *Bodhi- sattvacharyavatara* by the 12th century Tibetan Lama Thog-me Zang-po, be used as the basis for the translation. For the following year Geshe Ngawang Dhargyey, proceeded to give a word by word explanation of this text translated by Sharpa Tulku. It is on the basis of that teaching that this translation has been completed.

Chapters 1-8 and chapter 10 have been translated in verse form, corresponding to the stanzas of the root text. Where necessary, words have been added in brackets from the commentary. The ninth chapter, however, is presented in prose, frequently in the form of a dialogue between the Madhyamika school and other Buddhist and non-Buddhist tradition. Here, most of the commentary of Thog-me Zangpo has been included for the sake of clarifying the often cryptic style of the root text.

Stephen Batchelor
Switzerland, 1979.

A Guide to the
Bodhisattava's Way of Life

—◆—

Homage to all Buddha's and Bodhisattvas

CHAPTER I

The Benefits of the Awakening Mind[1]

1a

Respectfully I prostrate myself to the Sugatas
Who are endowed with the Dharmakaya,
As well as to their Noble Children
And to all who are worthy of veneration.

1b

Here I shall explain how to engage in the vows of the Buddha's
    Children,
The meaning of which I have condensed in accordance with the
    scriptures.

2

There is nothing here that has not been explained before
And I have no skill in the art of rhetoric;
Therefore, lacking any intention to benefit others,
I write this in order to acquaint it to my mind.

3

For due to acquaintance with what is wholesome,
The force of my faith may for a short while increase because of
    these (words).
If, however, these (words) are seen by others
Equal in fortune to myself, it may be meaningful (for them).

4

Leisure and endowment[2] are very hard to find;
And, since they accomplish what is meaningful for humanity,
If I do not take advantage of them now,
How will such a perfect opportunity come about again?

5

Just as a flash of lightning on a dark, cloudy night
For an instant brightly illuminates all,
Likewise in this world, through the might of Buddha,
A wholesome thought rarely and briefly appears.

6

Hence virtue is perpetually feeble,
The great strength of immorality being extremely intense,
And except for a Fully Awakening Mind
By what other virtue will it be overcome?

7

All the Buddhas who have contemplated for many aeons
Have seen it to be beneficial;
For by it the limitless masses of beings
Will quickly attain the supreme state of bliss.

8

Those who wish to destroy the many sorrows of (their) condi-
    tioned existence,
Those who wish (all beings) to experience a multitude of joys,
And those who wish to experience much happiness
Should never forsake the Awakening Mind.

9

The moment an Awakening Mind arises
In those fettered and weak in the jail of cyclic existence,
They will be named a 'Child of the Sugatas',
And will be revered by both humans and gods of the world.

10

It is like the supreme gold-making elixir,
For it transforms the unclean body we have taken
Into the priceless jewel of a Buddha-Form.
Therefore firmly seize this Awakening Mind.

11

Since the limitless mind of the Sole Guide of the World
Has upon thorough investigation seen its preciousness,
All beings wishing to be free from worldly abodes
Should firmly take hold of this precious Awakening Mind.

12

All other virtues are like plantain trees;
For after bearing fruit, they simply perish.
Yet the perennial tree of the Awakening Mind
Unceasingly bears fruit and thereby flourishes without end.

13

Like entrusting myself to a brave man when greatly afraid
By entrusting myself to this (Awakening Mind) I shall be swiftly
    liberated
Even if I have committed extremely unbearable wrongs.
Why then do the conscientious not devote themselves to this?

14

Just like the fire at the end of an age,
It instantly consumes all great wrongdoing.
Its unfathomable advantages were taught
To the disciple Sudhana by the wise Lord Maitreya.[3]

15

In brief, the Awakening Mind
Should be understood to be of two types;
The mind that aspires to awaken
And the mind that ventures to do so.

16

As is understood by the distinction
Between aspiring to go and (actually) going,
So the wise understand in turn
The distinction between these two.

17

Although great fruits occur in cyclic existence
From the mind that aspires to awaken,
An uninterrupted flow of merit does not ensue
As it does with the venturing mind.

18

And for those who have perfectly seized this mind,
With the thought never to turn away
From totally liberating
The infinite forms of life,

19

From that time hence,
Even while asleep or unconcerned,
A force of merit equal to the sky
Will perpetually ensue.

20

For the sake of those inclined towards the lesser (vehicle),
This was logically asserted
By the Tathagata himself
In *The Sutra Requested by Subahu.*[4]

21

If even the thought to relieve
Living creatures of merely a headache
Is a beneficial intention
Endowed with infinite goodness,

22

Then what need is there to mention
The wish to dispel their inconceivable misery,
Wishing every single one of them
To realize boundless good qualities?

23

Do even fathers and mothers
Have such a benevolent intention as this?
Do the gods and sages?
Does even Brahma have it?

24

If those beings have never before
Even dreamt of such an attitude
For their own sake,
How would it ever arise for the sake of others?

25

This intention to benefit all beings,
Which does not arise in others even for their own sake,
Is an extraordinary jewel of the mind,
And its birth is an unprecedented wonder.

26

How can I fathom the depths
Of the goodness of this jewel of the mind,
The panacea that relieves the world of pain
And is the source of all its joy?

27

If merely a benevolent intention
Excels veneration of the Buddhas,
Then what need to mention striving to make
All beings, without exception, happy?

28

Although wishing to be rid of misery,
They run towards misery itself.
Although wishing to have happiness,
Like an enemy they ignorantly destroy it.

29

For those who are deprived of happiness
And burdened with many sorrows,
It satisfies them with all joys,
Dispels all suffering,

30

And clears away confusion.
Where is there a comparable virtue?
Where is there even such a friend?
Where is there merit similar to this?

31

If whoever repays a kind deed
Is worthy of some praise,
Then what need to mention the Bodhisattvas
Who do good without it being asked of them?

32

The world honors as virtuous
One who sometimes gives a little, plain food
Disrespectfully to a few beings,
Which satisfies them for only half a day.

33

What need be said then of one
Who eternally bestows the peerless bliss of the Sugatas
Upon limitless numbers of beings,
Thereby fulfilling all their hopes?

34

The Buddha has said that whoever bears a harmful thought
Against a benefactor such as a Bodhisattva
Will remain in hell for as many aeons
As there were harmful thoughts.[5]

35

However, if a virtuous attitude should arise (in that regard),
Its fruits will multiply far more than that.
When Bodhisattvas greatly suffer they generate no negativity,
Instead their virtues naturally increase.

36

I bow down to the body of those
In whom the sacred precious mind is born.
I seek refuge in that source of joy
Who brings happiness even to those who bring harm.

CHAPTER II

Disclosure of Wrongdoing

1

In order to seize that precious mind
I offer now to the Tathagatas,
To the sacred Dharma, the stainless jewel,
And to the Disciples of Buddha, the Oceans of Excellence,

2

Whatever flowers and fruits there are,
And whatever kinds of medicine,
Whatever jewels exist in this world
And whatever clean, refreshing waters;

3

Likewise gem-encrusted mountains,
Forest groves, quiet and joyful places,
Heavenly trees bedecked with flowers
And trees with fruit-laden branches;

4

Fragrances of the celestial realms,
Incense, wishing trees and jewel trees,
Uncultivated harvests, and all ornaments
That are worthy of being offered;

5

Lakes and pools adorned with lotuses,
And the beautiful cry of wild geese,
Everything unowned
Within the limitless spheres of space;

6

Creating these things in my mind, I offer them
To the supreme beings, the Buddhas, as well as their Children,
O Compassionate Ones, think kindly of me
And accept these offerings of mine.

7

Having no merit, I am destitute,
And I have no other gifts to offer.
O Protectors, you who think of helping others,
By your power accept these for my sake.

8

Eternally shall I offer all my bodies
To the Conquerors and their Children,
Please accept me, you Supreme Heroes,
Respectfully shall I be your subject.

9

By being completely under your care,
I shall benefit all with no fears of conditioned existence;
I shall perfectly transcend my previous transgressions
And in the future shall commit no more.

10

To very sweetly-scented bathing chambers,
With brilliantly sparkling crystal floors
And exquisite pillars ablaze with gems,
With canopies above aglow with pearls,

11

I beseech the Tathagatas and their Children
To come and bathe their bodies
From many-jewelled vases, filled with waters scented and enticing,
To the accompaniment of music and song.

12

Let me dry their bodies with incomparable cloths
Clean and well-anointed with scent,
And then may I present these Holy Beings
With fragrant garments of suitable colors.

13

I adorn with manifold ornaments
And various raiments fine and smooth,
The Aryas Samantabhadra, Manjughosha,
Avalokiteshvara and all the others.

14

Just like polishing pure, refined gold
I anoint the Buddha's forms, which blaze with light,
With the choicest perfumes, whose fragrance permeates
A thousand million worlds.

15

And to the highest objects of giving, I offer
Beautiful, well-arranged garlands,
As well as enchanting, sweet-smelling flowers
Such as lilies, jasmine and lotus blooms.

16

Also, I send forth clouds of incense
Whose sweet aroma steals away the mind,
As well as celestial delicacies
Including a variety of foods and drinks.

17

I offer them jewelled lamps
Arranged on golden lotus buds;
Upon land sprinkled with scented water
I scatter delicate flower petals.

18

To those who have the nature of compassion,
I offer palaces resounding with melodious hymns,
Exquisitely illuminated by hanging pearls and gems
That adorn the infinities of space.

19

Eternally shall I offer to all the Buddhas
Jewelled umbrellas with golden handles
And exquisite ornaments embellished to the rims,
Standing erect, and their shapes beautiful to behold.

20

In addition, may a mass of offerings
Resounding with sweet and pleasing music,
(Like) clouds that appease the misery of all,
Each remaining (for as long as necessary),

21

And may a continuous rain
Of flowers and precious gems descend
Upon the reliquaries and the statues,
And upon all the jewels of Dharma.

22

In the same way as Manjughosha and others
Have made offerings to the Conquerors,
Similarly do I bestow gifts upon the Tathagatas,
The Protectors, their Children and all.

23

I glorify the Oceans of Excellence
With limitless verses of harmonious praise;
May these clouds of gentle eulogy
Constantly ascend to their presence.

24

With bodies as numerous
As all the atoms within the universe,
I prostrate to all the Buddhas of the three times,
The Dharma and the Supreme Community.

25

Likewise I prostrate to all the reliquaries,
To the bases of Awakening Mind,
To all learned abbots and masters
And to all the noble practitioners.

26

I seek refuge in all the Buddhas
Until I possess the essence of Awakening;
I seek refuge in Dharma
And in the assembly of Bodhisattvas.

27

With folded hands, I beseech
The Buddhas and Bodhisattvas,
Who possess the great compassion
And reside in all directions.

28

Throughout beginningless cyclic existence,
In this life and others,
Unknowingly, I committed transgressions
And ordered them to be done (by others).

29

Overwhelmed by the deception of ignorance
I rejoiced in what was done,
But now, seeing these mistakes,
From my heart I confess them to the Buddhas.

30

Whatever harmful acts of body, speech and mind
I have done, in a disturbed mental state,
Towards the three jewels of refuge,
My parents, my spiritual masters and others,

31

And all the grave wrongs done by me,
So thoroughly vile and polluted
With an abundance of faults,
I openly declare to the Guides of the World.

32

But I may well perish
Before all my transgressions have been purified,
So please protect me in such a way
As will swiftly and surely free me from them.

33

The untrustworthy Lord of Death
Waits not for things to be done or undone;
Whether I am sick or healthy,
This fleeting lifespan is unstable.

34

Leaving all, I must depart alone.
Yet through not having understood this,
I committed various kinds of wrongdoing
For the sake of my friends and foes.

35

My foes will become nothing.
My friends will become nothing.
I, too, will become nothing.
Likewise, all will become nothing.

36

Just like a dream experience,
Whatever things I enjoy
Will become a memory.
Whatever has passed will not be seen again.

37

Even within this brief life,
Many friends and foes have passed,
But whatever unbearable wrongdoing I committed for them
Remains ahead of me.

38

Thereby, through not having realized
That I shall suddenly vanish,
I committed so much wrong
Out of ignorance, lust and hate.

39

Remaining neither day nor night,
Life is always slipping by
And never getting any longer.
Why would death not come to one like me?

40

While I am lying in bed,
Although surrounded by my friends and relatives,
The feeling of life being severed
Will be experienced by me alone.

41

When seized by the messengers of death,
What benefit will friends and relatives afford?
My merit alone shall protect me then,
But upon that I have never relied.

42

O Protectors! I, so unconcerned,
Unaware of such terror as this,
Accumulated a great deal of negative action
For the sake of this transient life.

43

Petrified is the person
Today being led to a torture chamber.
With a dry mouth and dreadful, sunken eyes,
His entire appearance is transfigured.

44

What need to mention the tremendous despair
When stricken with the disease of great panic,
Being clasped by the physical forms
Of the frightful messengers of death?

45

"Who can afford me real protection
From this great horror?"
With terrified, bulging eyes agape
I shall search in every direction for refuge.

46

Upon seeing no refuge anywhere,
I shall become enveloped in gloom.
If there should be no protection there,
Then what shall I be able to do?

47

Therefore, I now seek refuge
In the Buddhas who protect the world,
Who strive to shelter all that lives
And, with great strength, eradicate all fear.

48

Likewise, I purely seek refuge
In the Dharma, which they have realized
Clears away the fears of cyclic existence,
And also in the assembly of Bodhisattvas.

49

I, trembling with fear,
Offer myself to Samantabhadra;
To Manjughosha, also,
I make a gift of my body.

50

To the Protector Avalokiteshvara,
Who infallibly acts with compassion,
I utter a mournful cry,
"Please protect this miscreant!"

51

In my search for refuge,
I cry from my heart
For Akashagarba, Ksitigarbha,
And all the Compassionate Protectors.

52

And I seek refuge in Vajrapani,
Upon the sight of whom all harmful beings,
Such as the messengers of death,
Flee in terror in all directions.

53

Previously I transgressed your advice,
But now, upon seeing this great fear,
I go to you for refuge.
By doing so, may this fear be swiftly cleared away.

54

If I need to comply with a doctor's advice
When frightened by a common illness,
Then how much more so when perpetually diseased
By the manifold agitations of desire and so forth.

55

And if all people living on this earth
Can be overcome by just one of these,
And if no other medicine to cure them
Is to be found elsewhere in the universe,

56

Then the intention not to act in accordance
With the advice of the All-knowing Physicians
That can uproot every misery
Is extremely bewildered and worthy of scorn.

57

If I need to be careful
Near a small, ordinary precipice,
Then how much more so near the one of deep duration
That drops for a thousand miles.

58

It is inappropriate to enjoy myself,
Thinking that today alone I shall not die,
For inevitably the time will come
When I shall become nothing.

59

Who can grant me fearlessness?
How can I be surely free from this?
If I shall inevitably become nothing,
How can I relax and enjoy myself?

60

What remains with me now
From the terminated experiences of the past?
Yet through my great attachment to them
I have been going against my spiritual master's advice.

61

Having departed from this life
And from all my friends and relatives,
If all alone I must go elsewhere
What is the use of making friends and enemies?

62

"How can I be surely freed
From unwholesomeness, the source of misery?"
Continuously, night and day,
I should only consider this.

63

Whatever has been done by me
Through ignorance and unknowing,
Be it the breaking of a vow
Or a deed by nature wrong,

64

I humbly confess it all
In the presence of the Protectors,
With folded hands, prostrating myself again and again,
My mind terrified by the misery (to-come).

65

I beseech all the Guides of the World
To please accept my transgressions and wrongs.
Since these are not good,
In the future I shall do them no more.

CHAPTER III

Full Acceptance of the Awakening Mind

1

Gladly do I rejoice
In the virtue that relieves the misery
Of all those in unfortunate states
And that gives happiness to the suffering.

2

I rejoice in that gathering of virtue
That is the cause for (the Arhat's) Awakening.
I rejoice in the definite freedom of embodied creatures
From the miseries of cyclic existence.

3

I rejoice in the Awakening of the Buddhas,
And also in the spiritual levels of their Children.

4

And with gladness I rejoice
In the ocean of virtue, for developing an Awakening Mind
That wishes all beings to be happy,
As well as in the deeds that bring them benefit.

5

With folded hands, I beseech
The Buddhas of all directions
To shine the lamp of Dharma
For all bewildered in misery's gloom.

6

With folded hands, I beseech
The Conquerors who wish to pass away
To please remain for countless aeons,
And not to leave the world in darkness.

7

Thus by the virtue collected
Through all that I have done,
May the pain of every living creature
Be completely cleared away.

8

May I be the doctor, the medicine
And may I be the nurse
For all sick beings in the world,
Until everyone is healed.

9

May a rain of food and drink descend
To clear away the pain of thirst and hunger,
And during the aeon of famine
May I myself change into food and drink.

10

May I become an inexhaustible treasure
For those who are poor and destitute;
May I turn into all things they could need
And be placed close beside them.

11

Without any sense of loss,
I shall give up my body and enjoyments
As well as all my virtues of the three times
For the sake of benefitting all.

12

By giving up all, sorrow is transcended
And my mind will realize the sorrowless state.
It is best that I (now) give everything to all beings
In the same way as I shall (at death).[6]

13

Having given this body up
For the pleasure of all living beings,
By killing, abusing and beating it,
May they always do as they please.

14

Although they may play with my body
And make it a source of jest and reproach,
Because I have given it up to them
What is the use of holding it dear?

15

Therefore, I shall let them do anything to it
That does not cause them any harm,
And when anyone encounters me
May it never be meaningless for them.

16

If, in those who encounter me,
A faithful or an angry thought arises,
May that eternally become the source
For fulfilling all their wishes.

17

May all who say bad things to me
Or cause me any other harm,
And those who mock and insult me
Have the fortune to fully awaken.

18

May I be a protector for those without one,
A guide for all travellers on the way;
May I be a bridge, a boat and a ship
For all who wish to cross (the water).

19

May I be an island for those who seek one,
And a lamp for those desiring light,
May I be a bed for all who wish to rest
And a slave for all who want a slave.

20

May I be a wishing jewel, a magic vase,
Powerful mantras and great medicine,
May I become a wish-fulfilling tree
And a cow of plenty for the world.

21

Just like space
And the great elements such as earth,
May I always support the lives
Of all the boundless creatures.

22

And until they pass away from pain,
May I also be the source of life
For all the realms of varied beings
That reach unto the ends of space.

23

Just as the previous Sugatas
Gave birth to an Awakening Mind,
And just as they successively dwelt
In the Bodhisattva practices;

24

Likewise, for the sake of all that lives
Do I give birth to an Awakening Mind,
And likewise shall I, too,
Successively follow the practices.

25

In order to further increase it from now on,
Those with discernment who have lucidly seized
An Awakening Mind in this way,
Should highly praise it in the following manner:

26

Today my life has (borne) fruit;
(Having) well obtained this human existence,
I've been born in the family of Buddha
And now am one of Buddha's Children.

27

Thus, whatever actions I do from now on
Must be in accord with the family.
Never shall I disgrace or pollute
This noble and unsullied race.

28

Just like a blindman
Discovering a jewel in a heap of rubbish,
Likewise, by some coincidence,
An Awakening Mind has been born within me.

29

It is the supreme ambrosia
That overcomes the sovereignty of death,
It is the inexhaustible treasure
That eliminates all poverty in the world.

30

It is the supreme medicine
That quells the world's disease.
It is the tree that shelters all beings
Wandering and tired on the path of conditioned existence.

31

It is the universal bridge
That leads to freedom from unhappy states of birth,
It is the dawning moon of the mind
That dispells the torment of disturbing conceptions.[7]

32

It is the great sun that finally removes
The misty ignorance of the world,
It is the quintessential butter
From the churning of the milk of Dharma.

33

For all those guests travelling on the path of conditioned existence
Who wish to experience the bounties of happiness,
This will satisfy them with joy
And actually place them in supreme bliss.

34

Today in the presence of all the Protectors
I invite the world to be guests
At (a festival of) temporary and ultimate delight.
May gods, demi-gods and all be joyful.

CHAPTER IV

Conscientiousness

1

Having firmly seized the Awakening Mind in this way,
Conqueror's Children must never waver;
Always should they exert themselves
To never stray from their practice.

2

In the case of reckless actions
Or of deeds not well considered,
Although a promise may have been made,
It is fit to reconsider whether I should do them or not.

3

But how can I ever withdraw
From what has been examined by the great wisdom
Of the Buddhas and the Bodhisattvas,
And even many times by me myself?

4

If, having made such a promise,
I do not put it into action,
Then by deceiving every living being,
What kind of rebirth shall I take?

5

If it has been taught (by the Buddha)
That those who do not give away
The smallest thing which they once intended to give
Will take rebirth as hungry ghosts;[8]

6

Then if I should deceive all beings,
After having sincerely invited them
To the unsurpassable bliss,
Shall I take a happy rebirth?

7

Only the Omniscient can discern
The manner of the action of those
Who give up the Awakening Mind but are freed;
It is beyond the scope of (ordinary) thought.

8

This, for a Bodhisattva,
Is the heaviest of downfalls,
For should it ever happen,
The welfare of all will be weakened.

9

And should others for even a single moment
Hinder or obstruct their wholesome (deeds),
By weakening the welfare of all,
There will be no end to their rebirth in lower states.

10

For if my being is impaired
By destroying the joy of even one creature,
Then what need is there to mention
Destroying the joy of creatures vast as space?[9]

11

Thus those who have the force of an Awakening Mind,
As well as the force of falling (from it),
Stay revolving within cyclic existence
And for a long time are hindered from reaching the Bodhisattva
    levels.

12

Therefore, just as I have promised
I shall respectfully accord my actions.
If from now on I make no effort,
I shall descend to lower and lower states.

13

Although for the benefit of every creature
Countless Buddhas have passed by,
I was not an object of their care
Because of my own mistakes.

14

And if I continue to act like this,
Again and again shall I undergo
(Suffering) in unhappy realms, sickness, bondage,
Laceration and the shedding of blood.

15

If the arising of the Tathagata,
Faith, the attainment of a human body,
And my being fit to cultivate virtue are scarce,
When will they be won again?

16

Although today I am healthy,
Well-nourished and unafflicted,
Life is momentary and deceptive;
The body is like an object on loan for but a minute.

17

With behavior such as this,
I shall not win a human body again,
And if this human form is not attained,
There will be solely wrongdoing and no virtue.

18

If when I have the chance to live a wholesome life
My actions are not wholesome,
Then what shall I be able to do
When confused by the misery of the lower realms?

19

And if I commit no wholesome deeds (there),
But readily amass much wrongdoing,
Then for a hundred million aeons
I shall not even hear the words "a happy life."

20

For these very reasons, the Buddha has said
That as difficult as it is for a turtle to insert its neck
Into a yoke adrift upon the vast ocean,
It is more difficult to attain the human state.[10]

21

If even by the transgression of one instant
An aeon may be spent in the deepest hell,
Then because of the transgressions I have gathered since
    beginningless time,
What need to mention my not going to a happy realm?

22

Yet having experienced merely that (rebirth in hell)
I shall still not be liberated;
For a while it is being experienced,
Other wrongdoing will be extensively produced.

23

So if, when having found leisure such as this,
I do not attune myself to what is wholesome,
There could be no greater deception,
And there could be no greater folly.

24

And if, having understood this,
I still foolishly continue to be slothful,
When the hour of death arrives,
Tremendous grief will rear its head.

25

Then if my body blazes for a long time
In the unbearable flames of hell,
Inevitably my mind will be tormented
By the fires of unendurable remorse.

26

Having found by some coincidence
This beneficial state that is so hard to find,
If now, while able to discriminate,
I once again am led into the hells,

27

Then as though I were hypnotized by a spell
I shall reduce this mind to nothing.
Even I do not know what is causing me confusion;
What is there dwelling inside me?

28

Although enemies such as hatred and craving
Have neither any arms nor legs,
And are neither courageous nor wise,
How have I, like a slave, been used by them?

29

For while they dwell within my mind
At their pleasure, they cause me harm,
Yet I patiently endure them without any anger;
But this is an inappropriate and shameful time for patience.

30

Should even all the gods and demi-gods
Rise up against me as my enemies,
They could not lead nor place me in
The roaring fires of deepest hell.

31

Yet the mighty foe, these disturbing conceptions,
In a moment can cast me amidst (those flames)
Which, when met, will cause not even the ashes
Of the king of mountains to remain.

32

All other enemies are incapable
Of remaining for such a length of time
As can my disturbing conceptions;
The enduring enemy has neither beginning nor end.

33

If I agreeably honor and entrust myself (to others),
They will bring me benefit and happiness,
But if I entrust myself to these disturbing conceptions,
In the future they will bring only misery and harm.

34

While in cyclic existence, how can I be joyful and unafraid
If, in my heart, I readily prepare a place
For this incessant enemy of long duration,
The sole cause for the increase of all that harms me?

35

And how shall I ever have happiness
If, in a net of attachment within my mind,
There dwell the guardians of the prison of cyclic existence,
These (disturbing conceptions) that become my butchers and
   tormentors in hell?

36

Therefore as long as this enemy is not slain with certainty before
    my very eyes,
I shall never give up exerting myself (towards that end).
Having become angry at someone who caused only slight and
    short-lived harm,
Self-important people will not sleep until their (enemy) is overcome.

37

And if while engaged in a violent battle,
The vigorous desire to conquer those whole disturbing concep-
    tions will naturally bring them suffering at death,
Men disregard the pain of being pierced by spears and arrows
And will not withdraw until the day is won;

38

Then what need to mention that I should not be faint-hearted
    and slothful,
Even if I am caused many hundreds of sufferings
When now I strive to definitely overcome my natural enemies,
(These disturbing conceptions) which are the constant source of
    my misery?

39

If even scars inflicted by meaningless enemies
Are worn upon the body like ornaments,
Then why is suffering a cause of harm to me
While impeccably striving to fulfill the great purpose?

40

If fishermen, hunters and farmers,
Thinking merely of their own livelihood,
Endure the sufferings of heat and cold,
Why am I not patient for the sake of the world's joy?

41

When I promised to liberate all beings,
Who dwell in the ten directions as far as the ends of space,
From their disturbing conceptions,
I myself was not yet freed from mine.

42

Thus, unaware of even my own capacity,
Was it not somewhat crazy to have spoken like that?
Yet as this is so, I must never withdraw
From vanquishing my disturbing conceptions.

43

And to do this will be my sole obsession:
Holding a strong grudge, I shall meet them in battle!
Yet disturbing conceptions such as these
Destroy disturbing conceptions and (for the time being) are not
    to be (abandoned).

44

It would be better for me to be burned,
To have my head cut off and to be killed,
Rather than ever bowing down
To those ever-present disturbing conceptions.

45

Common enemies, when expelled from one country,
Simply retire and settle down in another,
Though when their strength is recovered, they then return.
However, the way of this enemy, my disturbing conceptions, is
    not similar in this respect.

46

Deluded, disturbing conceptions! When forsaken by the eye of
    wisdom
And dispelled from my mind, where will you go?
Where will you dwell, in order to be able to injure me again (later)?
Weak-minded, I have been reduced to making no effort.

47

If these disturbing conceptions do not exist within the objects,
the sense organs, between the two nor elsewhere,
Then where do they exist and how do they harm the world?
They are like an illusion—thus I should dispel the fear within my
heart and strive resolutely for wisdom.
For no real reason, why should I suffer so much in hell?

48

Therefore, having thought about this well,
I should try to put these precepts into practice just as they have
been explained.
If the doctor's instructions are ignored,
How will a patient in need of a cure be healed by the medicine?

CHAPTER V

Guarding Alertness

1

Those who wish to guard their practice
Should very attentively guard their minds,
For those who do not guard their minds
Will be unable to guard their practice.

2

In this (world), unsubdued and crazed elephants
Are incapable of causing such harms
As the miseries of the deepest hell,
Which can be caused by the unleashed elephant of my mind.

3

However, if the elephant of my mind is firmly bound
On all sides by the rope of mindfulness,
All fears will cease to exist
And all virtues will come into my hand.

4

Tigers, lions, elephants, bears,
Snakes and all forms of enemies,
The guardians of the hell worlds,
Evil spirits and cannibals,

5

Will all be bound
By binding my mind alone,
And will all be subdued
By subduing my mind alone.[11]

6

The Perfect Teacher himself has shown
That, in this way, all fears
As well as all boundless miseries
Originate from the mind.

7

Who intentionally created
All the weapons for those in hell?
Who created the burning iron ground?
From where did all the women (in hell) ensue?

8

The Mighty One has said that all such things
Are (the workings of) a negative mind,
Hence within the three world spheres
There is nothing to fear other than my mind.[12]

9

If the perfection of generosity
Were the alleviation of the world's poverty,
Then since beings are still starving now,
In what manner did the previous Buddhas perfect it?

10

The perfection of generosity is said to be
The thought to give all beings everything,
Together with the fruit of such a thought;
Hence it is simply a state of mind.

11

Nowhere has the killing
Of fish and other creatures been eradicated;
For the attainment of (merely) the thought to forsake (such things)
Is explained as the perfection of moral discipline.

12

Unruly beings are as (unlimited) as space:
They cannot possibly all be overcome.
However, if I overcome thoughts of anger alone,
This will be equivalent to vanquishing all foes.

13

Where would I possibly find enough leather
With which to cover the surface of the earth?
Yet (wearing) leather just on the soles of my shoes
Is equivalent to covering the earth with it.

14

Likewise, it is not possible for me
To restrain the external course of things;
But should I restrain this mind of mine
What would be the need to restrain all else?

15

Although the development of merely a clear state of concentration
Can result in (taking birth in) Brahma's realm,
Physical and vocal actions cannot so result
When (accompanied) by weak (mental) conduct.

16

The Knower of Reality has said
That even if recitation and physical hardships
Are practiced for long periods of time,
They will be meaningless if the mind is distracted elsewhere.[13]

17

Even those who wish to find happiness and overcome misery
Will wander with no aim nor meaning
If they do not comprehend the secret of the mind—
The paramount significance of Dharma.

18

This being so,
I shall hold and guard my mind well.
Without the discipline of guarding the mind,
What use are many other disciplines?

19

Just as I would be attentive and careful of a wound
When amidst a bustling, uncontrolled crowd,
So I should always guard the wound of my mind
When dwelling among harmful people.

20

And if I am careful of a wound
Through fear of it being slightly hurt,
Then why do I not guard the wound of my mind
Through fear of being crushed by the mountains of hell?

21

Should I behave in such a way as this,
Then whether among harmful people
Or even in the midst of women,
The steady effort to control myself will not decline.

22

It is better to be without wealth,
Honor, body and livelihood,
And it is better to let other virtues deteriorate,
Rather than ever to let (the virtues of) the mind decline.

23

O you who wish to guard your minds,
I beseech you with folded hands:
Always exert yourselves to guard
Mindfulness and alertness![14]

24

People who are disturbed by sickness
Have no strength to do anything (useful),
Likewise, those whose minds are disturbed by confusion
Have no strength to do anything (wholesome).

25

Whatever has been learned, contemplated and meditated upon
By those whose minds lack alertness,
Just like water in a leaking vase,
It will not be retained in their memory.

26

Even those who have much learning,
Faith and willing perseverance
Will become defiled by a (moral) fall
Due to the mistake of lacking alertness.

27

The thieves of unalertness,
In following upon the decline of mindfulness,
Will steal even the merits I have firmly gathered
(So that) I shall then proceed to lower realms.

28

This host of thieves, who are my own disturbing conceptions,
Will search for a good opportunity;
Having found it, they will steal my virtue
And destroy (the attainment of) life in a happy realm.

29

Therefore, I shall never let mindfulness depart
From the doorway of my mind.
If it goes, I should recall the misery of the lower realms,
And firmly re-establish it there.

30

Through staying in the company of spiritual masters,
Through the instructions of abbots and through fear,
Mindfulness will easily be generated
In fortunate people who practice with respect.

31

"I am ever dwelling in the presence
Of all the Buddhas and Bodhisattvas
Who are always endowed
With unobstructed vision."

32

By thinking in this way,
I shall mindfully develop a sense of shame, respect and fear.
Also through doing this,
Recollection of the Buddha will repeatedly occur.

33

When mindfulness is set with the purpose
Of guarding the doorway of the mind,
Then alertness will come about
And even that which had gone will return.

34

When, just as I am about (to act),
I see that my mind is tainted (with defilement),
At such a time I should remain
Unmoveable, like a piece of wood.

35

Never should I look around
Distractedly for no purpose;
With a resolute mind
I should always keep my eyes cast downwards.

36

In order to relax the gaze,
For a short while I should look around,
And if someone appears in my field of vision
I should look at them and say, "Welcome."

37

To check if there is any danger on the path
I should look again and again in all four directions.
To rest, I should turn my head around
And then look behind me.

38

Having examined both ahead and behind
I should proceed to either come or go.
Being aware of the necessity (for such mindful alertness)
I should behave like this in all situations.

39

(Once) having prepared for an action with the thought,
"My body will remain in such a way,"
Then periodically I should look to see
How the body is being maintained.

40

With the utmost effort I should check
To see that the crazed elephant of my mind
Is not wandering off, but is bound
To the great pillar of thinking about Dharma.

41

Those who strive by all means for concentration
Should not wander off even for a moment;
By thinking, "How is my mind behaving?"
They should closely analyse their mind.

42

However, if I am unable to do this
When afraid or involved in celebrations, then I should relax.
Likewise, it has been taught that at times of giving
One may be neutral to (certain aspects of) moral discipline.[15]

43

I should undertake whatever deed I have intended to do,
And think of doing nothing other than it.
With my mind applied to that task,
I should set about for the time being to accomplish it.

44

By acting in this way all will be done well,
But (by acting) otherwise, neither (action) will be done.
Likewise, there will be no increase in the proximate disturbing
      conceptions
That come from a lack of alertness.

45

If I happen to be present
While a senseless conversation is taking place,
Or if I happen to see some kind of spectacular show,
I should abandon attachment towards it.

46

If, for no reason, I start digging the earth,
Picking at the grass or drawing patterns on the ground,
Then by recalling the advice of the Buddhas,
I should immediately stop out of fear.

47

Whenever I have the desire
To move my body or to say something,
First of all I should examine my mind
And then, with steadiness, act in the proper way.

48

Whenever there is attachment in my mind
And whenever there is the desire to be angry,
I should not do anything nor say anything,
But remain like a piece of wood.

49

Whenever I have distracted thoughts, the wish to verbally be-
   little others,
Feelings of self-importance or self-satisfaction;
When I have the intention to describe the faults of others,
Pretension and the thought to deceive others;

50

Whenever I am eager for praise
Or have the desire to blame others;
Whenever I have the wish to speak harshly and cause disputes;
At (all) such times I should remain like a piece of wood.

51

Whenever I desire material gain, honor or fame;
Whenever I seek attendants or a circle of friends,
And when in my mind I wish to be served;
At (all) these times I should remain like a piece of wood.

52

Whenever I have the wish to decrease or to stop working for others
And the desire to pursue my welfare alone,
If (motivated by such thoughts,) a wish to say something occurs,
At these times I should remain like a piece of wood.

53

Whenever I have impatience, laziness, cowardice,
Shamelessness or the desire to talk nonsense;
If thoughts of partiality arise,
At these times, too, I should remain like a piece of wood.

54

Having in this way examined their minds for disturbing concep-
tions
And for thoughts that strive for meaningless things,
The courageous (Bodhisattvas) should hold their minds steady
Through (the application of) remedial forces.

55

Being very resolute and faithful,
Steady, respectful, polite,
With a sense of shame, apprehensive and peaceful,
I should strive to make others happy.

56

I should not be disheartened by all the whims
Of the childish who are in discord with one another;
I should know these to arise in their minds due to disturbing
conceptions
And therefore be kind (towards them).

57

In doing that which by nature is not unwholesome
Both for the sake of myself and other sentient beings
I should always hold my mind fast,
(Acting) like an apparition, with no sense of self.

58

By thinking again and again
That after a long time I have won the greatest leisure,
Likewise, I should hold my mind
As utterly unshakeable as the king of mountains.

59

If, mind, you are not made unhappy
When this body is dragged and tossed about
By vultures greedy for flesh,
Then why are you so concerned about it now?

60

Holding this body as "mine",
Why, mind, do you guard it so?
Since you and it are separate,
What use can it be to you?

61

Why, confused mind,
Do you not hold onto a clean, wooden form?
Just what is the point of guarding
This putrid, dirt-filled machine?

62

First of all, mentally separate
The layers of skin (from the flesh)
And then with the scalpel of discrimination
Separate the flesh from the skeletal frame;

63

And, having split open even the bones,
Look right down into the marrow.
While examining this, ask yourself,
"Where is its essence?"

64

If, even when searching with such effort
You can apprehend no essence,
Then why with so much attachment
Are you still guarding this body now?

65

What use is this body to you
If its dirty insides are unfit for you to eat,
If its blood is not fit to drink
And if its intestines are not fit to be sucked?

66

At second best, it is only fit to be guarded
In order to feed the vultures and jackals.
(Truly) this body of a human being
Should only be employed (in the practice of virtue).

67

Yet should you instead guard it (with attachment),
Then what will you be able to do
When it is stolen by the unsympathetic Lord of Death
And given to the dogs and birds?

68

If servants are not given clothing and so forth
When they are unable to be employed,
Then why do you exhaust yourself looking after the flesh alone
When, even though caring for the body, it goes elsewhere?

69

Now having paid my body its wages,
I shall engage it in making my life meaningful.
However, if my body is of no benefit,
Then I shall not give it anything.

70

I should conceive of my body as a boat,
A mere support for coming and going,
And in order to benefit all others
Transform it into a wish-fulfilling body.

71

Now, while there is freedom to act,
I should always present a smiling face
And cease to frown and look angry;
I should be a friend and counsel of the world.

72

I should desist from inconsiderately and noisily
Moving around chairs and so forth,
As well as from violently opening doors;
I should always delight in humility.

73

The stork, the cat and the thief,
By moving silently and carefully,
Accomplish what they desire to do;
A Bodhisattva, too, should always behave in this way.

74

With respect, I should gratefully accept
Unsought-after words that are of benefit,
And that wisely advise and admonish me.
At all times, I should be the pupil of everyone.

75

I should say, "Well said," to all those
Who speak (Dharma) well,
And if I see someone doing good,
I should praise them and be well pleased.

76

I should discreetly talk about the good qualities (of others)
And repeat those (that others) recount.
If my own good qualities are spoken about,
I should just know and be aware that I have them.

77

All deeds (of others) are the source of a joy
That would be rare even if it could be bought with money.
Therefore, I should be happy in finding this joy
In the good things that are done by others.

78

(Through doing this) I shall suffer no losses in this life
And in future lives shall find great happiness.
But the fault (of disliking their good qualities) will make me
    unhappy and miserable,
And in future lives I shall find great suffering.

79

When talking, I should speak from my heart on what is relevant,
Making the meaning clear and the speech pleasing.
I should not speak out of desire or hatred,
But in gentle tones and in moderation.

80

When beholding someone with my eyes,
Thinking, "I shall fully awaken
Through depending upon this being,"
I should look at that person with love and an open heart.

81

Always being motivated by great aspiration,
Or being motivated by the remedial forces,
If I work in the fields of excellence, benefit and misery,[16]
Great virtues will come about.

82

Endowed with wisdom and joy,[17]
I should undertake all that I (intend to) do.
I (need) not depend upon anyone else
In any actions that I undertake.

83

The perfections such as generosity
Are progressively more exalted,
But for a little (morality) I should not forsake a great (gift).
Principally, I should consider what will be of the most benefit
    for others.

84

When this is well understood,
I should always strive for the welfare of others.
The Far-Seeing Merciful Ones have allowed (a Bodhisattva)
To do some actions that (for others) were forbidden.

85

I should divide my food amongst those who have fallen to lower
   realms,
Those without protection, and practitioners,
And eat merely what is sufficient for myself.
Except for the three robes, I may give away all.

86

This body, which is being used for the sacred Dharma,
Should not be harmed for only slight benefit.
By behaving in this way,
The wishes of all beings will be quickly fulfilled.

87

Those who lack the pure intention of compassion
Should not give their body away.
Instead, both in this and future lives,
They should give it to the cause of fulfilling the great purpose.

88

The Dharma should not be explained to those who lack respect,
To those who, like the sick, wear cloth around their heads,
To those holding umbrellas, sticks or weapons,
To those with covered heads,

89

Nor to a woman unaccompanied by a man.
The vast and profound should not be taught to lesser beings,
(Although) I should always pay equal respect
To the Dharmas of the lesser and higher beings.

90

I should not communicate the Dharma of a lesser being
To one who is a vessel for the vast Dharma.
I must not forsake the (Bodhisattva's) way of life,
Nor mislead others by means of sutras or mantras.

91

When I spit or throw away the stick for (cleaning) my teeth,
I should cover it up (with earth).
Also it is shameful to urinate and so forth
In water or on land used by others.

92

When eating I should not fill my mouth,
Eat noisily or with my mouth wide open.
I should not sit with my legs outstretched,
Nor rub my hands together.

93

I should not sit alone in vehicles, upon beds,
Nor in the same room with the women of others.
(In brief,) having observed or inquired about what is proper,
I should not do anything that would be disliked by the people of
    the world.

94

I should not give directions with one finger,
But instead indicate the way
Respectfully with my right arm,
With all my fingers fully outstretched.

95

Nor should I wildly wave my arms about,
But should make my point
With slight gestures and a snap of my fingers.
Otherwise, I shall lose control.

96

Just as the Buddha lay down to pass away,
So should I lie in the desired direction (when going to sleep).
And first of all, with alertness,
Make the firm decision to quickly rise again.

97

(Although I am unable to practice all)
The limitless varieties of Bodhisattva conduct,
I should certainly practice as much as (has been mentioned here)
Of this conduct that trains the mind.

98

Three times by day and three times by night
I should recite *The Sutra of the Three Heaps;*[18]
For by relying upon the Buddhas and the Awakening Mind
My remaining downfalls will be purified.

99

Whatever I am doing in any situation,
Whether for myself or for the benefit of others,
I should strive to put into practice
Whatever has been taught for that situation.

100

There is no such thing as something
That is not learned by a Bodhisattva,
Thus if I am skilled in living in this way
Nothing will be non-meritorious.

101

Whether directly or indirectly, I should not do anything
That is not for the benefit of others.
Solely for the sake of sentient beings,
I should dedicate everything towards Awakening.

102

Never, even at the cost of my life,
Should I forsake a spiritual friend
Who is wise in the meaning of the great vehicle,
And who is a great Bodhisattva practitioner.

103

I should practice entrusting myself to my spiritual master
In the manner taught in *The Biography of Shrisambhava*.[19]
This and other advice spoken by the Buddha
I can understand through reading the sutras.

104

I should read the sutras
Because it is from them that the practices appear.
To begin with, I should look at
The Sutra of Akashagarba.

105

In addition I should definitely read
The Compendium of all Practices[20] again and again,
Because what is to be constantly practiced
Is very well and extensively shown there.

106

Also I should sometimes look at
The condensed *Compendium of All Sutras*.
And I should make an effort to study
The works by the same two (titles) composed by the exalted
    Nagarjuna.

107

I should do whatever is not forbidden in those (works).
And when I see a practice there,
I should impeccably put it into action,
In order to guard the minds of worldly people.

108

The defining characteristic of guarding alertness,
In brief, is only this;
To examine again and again
The condition of my body and mind.

109

Therefore, I shall put this way of life into actual practice,
For what can be achieved by merely talking about it?
Will the sick receive benefit
Merely by reading the medical texts?

Chapter VI

Patience

1

Whatever wholesome deeds,
Such as venerating the Buddhas and generosity,
That have been amassed over a thousand aeons
Will all be destroyed in one moment of anger.

2

There is no transgression like hatred,
And no fortitude like patience.
Thus I should strive in various ways
To meditate on patience.

3

My mind will not experience peace
If it fosters painful thoughts of hatred.
I shall find no joy or happiness;
Unable to sleep, I shall feel unsettled.

4

A master who has hatred
Is in danger of being killed
Even by those who, for their wealth and happiness,
Depend upon the master's kindness.

5

By it, friends and relatives are disheartened;
Though drawn by my generosity, they will not trust me;
In brief, there is nobody
Who lives happily with anger.

6

Hence the enemy, anger,
Creates sufferings such as these,
But whoever assiduously overcomes it
Finds happiness now and hereafter.

7

Having found its fuel of mental unhappiness
In the prevention of what I wish for,
And in doing what I do not want,
Hatred increases and then destroys me.

8

Therefore, I should totally eradicate
The fuel of this enemy;
For this enemy has no other function
Than that of causing me harm.

9

Whatever befalls me,
I shall not disturb my mental joy;
For having been made unhappy, I shall not accomplish what I wish,
And my virtues will decline.

10

Why be unhappy about something
If it can be remedied?
And what is the use of being unhappy about something
If it cannot be remedied?

11

For myself and for my friends
I want no suffering, no disrespect,
No harsh words and nothing unpleasant;
But for my enemies, it is the opposite.

12

The causes of happiness sometimes occur
But the causes for suffering are frequent.
Without suffering, there is no renunciation.
Therefore, mind, you should stand firm.

13

If some ascetics and the people of Karnapa
Endure the pain of cuts and burns for no reason,
Then for the sake of liberation
Why have I no courage?

14

There is nothing whatsoever
That is not made easier through acquaintance.
So through becoming acquainted with small harms,
I should learn to patiently accept greater harms.

15

Who has not seen this to be so, with trifling sufferings
Such as the bites of snakes and insects,
Feelings of hunger and thirst,
And with such minor things as rashes?

16

I should not be impatient
With heat and cold, wind and rain,
Sickness, bondage and beatings;
For if I am, the harm they cause me will increase.

17

Some, when they see their own blood,
Become especially brave and steady,
But some, when they see the blood of others,
Faint and fall unconscious.

18

These (reactions) come from the mind
Being either steady or timid.
Therefore, I should disregard harms caused to me,
And not be affected by suffering.

19

Even when the wise are suffering
Their minds remain very lucid and undefiled;
For when war is being waged against the disturbing conceptions,
Much harm is caused at the time of battle.

20

The victorious warriors are those
Who, having disregarded all suffering,
Vanquish the foes of hatred and so forth;
(Common warriors) slay only corpses.

21

Furthermore, suffering has good qualities:
Through being disheartened with it, arrogance is dispelled,
Compassion arises for those in cyclic existence,
Negativity is shunned and joy is found in virtue.

22

As I do not become angry
With great sources of suffering such as jaundice,
Then why be angry with animate creatures?
They, too, are provoked by conditions.

23

Although they are not wished for,
These sicknesses arise;
And likewise, although they are not wished for,
These disturbing conceptions forcibly arise.

24

Without thinking, "I shall be angry,"
People become angry with no resistance,
And without thinking, "I shall produce myself,"
Likewise anger itself is produced.

25

All mistakes that occur
And all the various kinds of wrongdoing
Arise through the force of conditions;
They do not govern themselves.

26

These conditions that assemble together
Have no intention to produce anything,
And neither does their product
Have the intention to be produced.

27

That which is asserted as Primal Substance[21]
And that which is imputed as a Self,[22]
(Since they are unproduced,) do not arise after having purpose-
    fully thought,
"I shall arise (in order to cause harm)."

28

If they are unproduced and non-existent,
Then whatever wish they have to produce (harm will also not
    exist).
Since (this Self) would permanently apprehend its object,
It follows that it would never cease to do so.

29

Furthermore, if the Self were permanent,
It would clearly be devoid of action, like space.
So even if it met with other conditions,
How could its unchanging (nature) be affected?

30

Even if when acted upon (by other conditions) it remains as before,
Then what could actions do to it?
Thus if I say that this (condition) acts upon (a permanent Self),
How could the two ever be (causally) related?

31

Hence everything is governed by other factors (which in turn)
    are governed by (others),
And in this way nothing governs itself.
Having understood this, I should not become angry
With phenomena, which are like apparitions.

32

-(If everything is unreal, like an apparition,) then who is there to
    restrain what (anger)?
Surely (in this case) restraint would be inappropriate-
It would not be inappropriate, because (conventionally) I must
    maintain
That in dependence upon restraining (anger), the stream of
    suffering is severed.

33

So when one sees an enemy or even a friend
Committing an improper action,
By thinking that such things arise from conditions
I shall remain in a happy frame of mind.

34

If things were brought into being by choice, ✓
Then since no one wishes to suffer,
Suffering would not occur
To any embodied creature.

35

Through not being careful,
People even harm themselves with thorns and other things,
And for the sake of obtaining women and the like,
They become obsessed and deprive themselves of food.

36

And there are some who injure themselves
Through the unmeritorious deeds
Of hanging themselves, leaping from cliffs,
Eating poison and unhealthy food.

37

If, when under the influence of disturbing conceptions,
People will even kill their treasured selves,
How can they be expected not to cause harm
To the bodies of other living beings?

38

Even if I cannot develop compassion for all such people
Who, through the arisal of disturbing conceptions,
Set out to try and kill me and so forth,
The last thing I should do is to become angry with them.

39

Even if it were the nature of the childish
To cause harm to other beings,
It would still be incorrect to be angry with them,
For this would be like begrudging fire for having the nature to
    burn.

40

And even if the fault were temporary
In they who are by nature reliable, good
It would still be incorrect to be angry,
For this would be like begrudging space for allowing smoke to
    arise in it.

41

If I become angry with the wielder,
Although I am actually harmed by the stick,
Then since the perpetrator, too, is secondary, being in turn
    incited by hatred,
I should be angry with the hatred instead.

42

Previously, I must have caused similar harm
To other sentient beings.
Therefore, it is right for this harm to be returned
To me, who caused injury to others.

43

Both the weapon and my body
Are the causes of my suffering.
Since the other gave rise to the weapon, and I to the body,
With whom should I be angry?

44

If, in blind attachment, I cling
To this suffering abscess of a human form
Which cannot bear to be touched,
With whom should I be angry when it is hurt?

45

It is the fault of the childish that they are hurt,
For although they do not wish to suffer,
They are greatly attached to its causes.
So why should they be angry with others?

46

Just like the guardians of the hell worlds
And the forest of razor-sharp leaves,
So is this (suffering) produced by my actions;
With whom therefore should I be angry?

47

Having been instigated by my own actions,
Those who cause me harm come into being.
If by these (actions) they should fall into hell,
Surely isn't it I who am destroying them?

48

In depending upon them, I purify many transgressions
By patiently accepting the harms that they cause.
But in depending upon me, they will fall
Into hellish pain for a very long time.

49

So since I am causing harm to them
And they are benefitting me,
Why, unruly mind, do you become angry
In such a mistaken manner?

50

If my mind has the noble quality (of patience),
I shall not go to hell.
Although I am protecting myself (in this way),
How will it be so for them?

51

Nevertheless, should I return the harm,
It will not protect them either.
By doing so my conduct will deteriorate,
And hence this fortitude will be destroyed.

52

Since my mind is not physical
In no way can anyone destroy it,
But through its being greatly attached to my body
It is caused harm by (physical) suffering.

53

Since disrespect, harsh speech
And unpleasant words
Do not cause any harm to my body,
Why, mind, do you become so angry?

54

-Because others will dislike me-
But since it will not devour me,
Either in this or in another life,
Why do I not want this (dislike)?

55

-Because it will hinder my wordly gain-
Even if I do not want this,
I shall have to leave my worldly gains behind
And my wrongdoing alone will remain unmoved.

56

Thus it is better that I die today
Than live a long but wicked life;
For even if people like me should live a long time,
There will always be the suffering of death.

57

Suppose someone should awaken from a dream
In which they experienced one hundred years of happiness,
And suppose another should awaken from a dream
In which they experienced just one moment of happiness;

58

For both of these people who have awoken,
That happiness will never return.
Similarly, whether my life has been long or short,
At the time of death it will be finished like this.

59

Although I may live happily for a long time
Through obtaining a great deal of material wealth,
I shall go forth empty-handed and destitute
Just like having been robbed by a thief.

60

Surely material wealth will enable me to live,
And then I shall be able to consume transgressions and do good-
But if I am angry on account of it
Will not my merit be consumed and transgressions increase?

61

And what use will be the life
Of one who only commits wrongdoing,
If, for the sake of material gain,
One causes (the merits needed for) life to degenerate?

62

-Surely I should be angry with those
Who say unpleasant things that weaken other beings' (confidence in me)-
In the same way, why am I not angry
With people who say unpleasant things about others?

63

If I can patiently accept this lack of confidence
Because it is related to someone else,
Then why am I not patient with unpleasant words (about myself),
Since they are related to the arising of disturbing conceptions?

64

Should others talk badly of or even destroy
Holy images, reliquaries and the sacred Dharma,
It is improper for me to resent it,
For the Buddhas can never be injured.

65

I should prevent anger arising towards those
Who injure my spiritual masters, relatives and friends.
Instead I should see, as in the manner shown before,
That such things arise from conditions.

66

Since embodied creatures are injured
By both animate beings and inanimate objects,
Why only bear malice to the animate?
It follows that I should patiently accept all harm.

67

Should one person ignorantly do wrong,
And another ignorantly become angry (with the wrongdoer),
Who would be at fault?
And who would be without fault?

68

Why did I previously commit those actions,
Because of which, others now cause me harm?
Since everything is related to my actions,
Why should I bear malice towards these (enemies)?

69

When I have seen this to be so,
I should strive for what is meritorious
(In order to) certainly bring about
Loving thoughts between all.

70

For example, when a fire in one house
Has moved into another house,
It is right to get rid of straw and such things
That will cause the fire to spread.

71

Likewise, when the fire of hatred spreads
To whatever my mind is attached to,
I should immediately get rid of it
For fear of my merit being burned.

72

Why is a person condemned to death not fortunate
If they are released after having a hand cut off?
Why am I who am experiencing human misery not fortunate
If by that I am spared from (the agonies of) hell?

73

If I am unable to endure
Even the mere sufferings of the present,
Then why do I not restrain myself from being angry,
Which will be the source of hellish misery?

74

For the sake of satisfying my desires,
I have suffered numerous burnings in hell;
But by those actions, I neither fulfilled the purpose
Of myself nor others.

75

Yet now, since great meaning will accrue
From harm which is not even (a fraction) of that,
I should indeed be solely joyful
Towards such suffering that dispels the harms of all.

76

Should someone else find joyous happiness
In praising (my enemy) as an excellent person,
Why, mind, do you not praise them, too,
And likewise make yourself happy?

77

That joyous happiness of yours
Would be a source of joy, not something prohibited,
A precept given by the Excellent Ones
And a supreme (means) for assembling others.

78

It is said that others are made happy through (being praised) in
this way.
If in this way, you do not want (them to have) this happiness,
Then, (since it makes them happy), you should cease giving
wages and the like (to your servants).
However, you would be adversely affected both in this and
future lives.

79

When people describe my own good qualities
I want others to be happy too
But when they describe the good qualities of others
I do not wish to be happy myself.

80

Having generated the Awakening Mind
Through wishing all beings to be happy,
Why should I become angry
If they find some happiness themselves?

81

If I wish for all sentient beings to become
Buddhas worshipped throughout the three realms,
Then why am I tormented
When I see them receiving merely mundane respect?

82

If a relative for whom I am caring,
And to whom I must give many things,
Should be able to find their own livelihood,
Wouldn't I be happy, rather than angry?

83

If I do not wish for beings to have even this,
How can I wish for them to awaken?
And where is there an Awakening Mind
In one who becomes angry when others receive things?

84

What does it matter if (my enemy) is given something or not?
Whether they obtain it
Or whether it remains in the benefactor's house,
In either case, I shall get nothing.

85

So why, by becoming angry, do I throw away my merits,
The faith (others have in me) and my good qualities?
Tell me, why am I not angry (with myself)
For not having the causes for gain?

86

Let alone not having any remorse
About the wrongs that you committed, (O mind,)
Why do you wish to compete with others
Who have committed meritorious deeds?

87

Even if your enemy is made unhappy,
What is there for you to be joyful about?
Your merely wishing (for them to be hurt)
Did not cause them to be injured.

88

And even if the enemy does suffer as you had wished,
What is there for you to be joyful about?
If you say, "For I shall be satisfied,"
How could there be anything more wretched than that?

89

This hook cast by the fishermen of disturbing conceptions
Is unbearably sharp. Having been caught on it,
It is certain that I shall be cooked
In cauldrons by the guardians of hell.

90

The honour of praise and fame
Will not turn into merit or life;
It will give me neither strength nor freedom from sickness,
And will not provide any physical happiness.

91

If I were aware of what held meaning for me,
What value would I find in these things?
If all I want is (a little) mental happiness,
I should devote myself to gambling, drinking and so forth.

92

If, for the sake of fame,
I give away my wealth or get myself killed,
What can the mere words (of fame) do then?
Once I have died, to whom will they give pleasure?

93

When their sandcastles collapse,
Children howl in despair;
Likewise, when my praise and reputation decline,
My mind becomes like a little child.

94

Since short-lived sounds are inanimate,
They cannot possibly think of praising me.
-But as it makes (the bestower of praise) happy,
(My) reputation is a source of pleasure (for me)-

95

Whether this praise is directed at myself or someone else
How shall I be benefitted by the joy (of the one who bestows it)?
Since that joy and happiness is theirs alone,
I shall not obtain even a part of it.

96

If I do find happiness in their happiness,
Then surely I should feel the same way towards all?
And if this were so, then why am I unhappy
When others find pleasure in that which brings them joy?

97

Therefore the happiness that arises
From thinking, "I am being praised," is invalid.
It is only the behaviour of a child.

98

Praise and so forth distract me,
And also undermine my disillusion (with cyclic existence);
I start to envy those who have good qualities,
And all the very best is destroyed.

99

Therefore, are not those who are closely involved
In destroying my praise and the like,
Also involved in protecting me
From falling into the unfortunate realms?

100

I, who am striving for freedom,
Do not need to be bound by material gain and honour.
So why should I be angry
With those who free me from this bondage?

101

Those who wish to cause me suffering
Are like Buddhas bestowing waves of blessing.
As they open the door for my not going to an unfortunate realm,
Why should I be angry with them?

102

-But what if someone should obstruct my gaining merit?-
With them, too, it is incorrect to be angry;
For since there is no fortitude similar to patience,
Surely I should put it into practice.

103

If due to my own failings,
I am not patient with this (enemy),
Then it is only I who am preventing myself
From practicing this cause for gaining merit.

104

If without it, something does not occur,
And if with it, it does comes to be,
Then since this (enemy) would be the cause of (patience)
How can I say that (the enemy) prevents it?

105

A beggar is not an obstacle to generosity
When I am giving something away,
And I cannot say that those who give ordination
Are an obstacle to becoming ordained.

106

There are indeed many beggars in this world,
But scarce are those who inflict harm;
For if I have not injured others,
Few beings will cause me harm.

107

Therefore, just like treasure appearing in my house
Without any effort on my part to obtain it,
I should be happy to have enemies
For they assist me in my conduct of Awakening.

108

Because I am able to practice (patience) with them,
They are worthy of being given
The very first fruits of my patience,
For in this way, they are the cause of it.

109

-But why should my enemy be venerated,
who has no intention for me to practice patience?-
Then why venerate the sacred Dharma?
(It too has no intention) but is a fit cause for practice.

110

-But surely my enemies are not to be venerated
For they intend to cause me harm-
Then how could patience be practiced
If, like doctors, people always strove to do me good?

111

Thus, since patient acceptance is produced
In dependence upon (one with) a very hateful mind,
That person should be worthy of veneration just like the sacred
     Dharma,
Because they are a cause of patience.

112

Therefore the Mighty One has said
That the field of sentient beings is (similar to) a Buddha-field,[23]
For many who have pleased them
Have thereby reached perfection.

113

A Buddha's qualities are gained
From the sentient beings and the Conquerors alike,
So why do I not respect them
In the same way as I respect the Conquerors?

114

(Of course) they are not similar in the quality of their intentions
But only in the fruits (that they produce);
So it is in this respect that they have excellent qualities
And are therefore (said to be) equal.

115

Whatever (merit comes from) venerating one with a loving mind
Is due to the eminence of sentient beings.
And in the same way, the merit of having faith in Buddha
Is due to the eminence of Buddha.

116

Therefore, they are asserted to be equal
In the share they have in establishing Buddha-qualities.
Yet none of them are equal (in good qualities)
With the Buddhas who are boundless Oceans of Excellence.

117

Even if the three realms were offered,
It would be insufficient in paying veneration
To those few beings in whom a mere share of the good qualities
Of the Unique Assemblage of Excellence appear.

118

Thus since sentient beings have a share
In giving rise to the supreme Buddha-qualities,
Surely it is correct to venerate them
As they are similar in merely this respect?

119

Furthermore, what way is there to repay (the Buddhas)
Who grant immeasurable benefit
And who befriend the world without pretension,
Other than by pleasing sentient beings?

120

Therefore, since benefitting these beings will repay
Those who give their bodies and enter the deepest hell for their
    sake,
I shall behave impeccably in all (that I do)
Even if they cause me a great deal of harm.

121

When for their sake, those who are my Lords
Have no regard even for their own bodies,
Then why am I the fool so full of self-importance?
Why do I not act like a servant towards them?

122

Because of their happiness, the Conquerors are delighted.
However, if they are harmed (the Conquerors) are displeased.
Hence by pleasing them I shall delight the Conquerors,
And by harming them I shall hurt the Conquerors.

123

Just as desirable sense-objects would give my mind no pleasure
If my body was ablaze with fire,
Likewise, when living creatures are in pain
There is no way for the Compassionate Ones to be pleased.

124

Therefore, as I have caused harm to living beings,
Today I openly declare all my unwholesome acts
That have brought displeasure to the Compassionate Ones.
Please bear with me, O Lords, for this displeasure I have caused
    you.

125

From now on, in order to delight the Tathagatas
I shall serve the universe and definitely cease (to cause harm).
Although many beings may kick and stamp upon my head,
Even at the risk of dying, may I delight the Protectors of the
    World (by not retaliating).

126

There is no doubt that those with the nature of compassion
Regard all these beings (the same) as themselves.
Furthermore, those who see (this Buddha nature) as the nature
  of sentient beings also see the Buddhas themselves;
Why then do I not respect (sentient beings)?

127

(Pleasing living beings) delights the Tathagatas
And perfectly accomplishes my own purpose as well.
In addition, it dispels the pain and misery of the universe,
Therefore I should always practice it.

128

For example, should some of the king's men
Cause harm to many people,
Farsighted ones would not return the harm
Even if they were able (to do so).

129

For they see that (these men) are not alone
But are supported by the might of the king.
Likewise, I should not underestimate
Weak beings who cause me a little harm;

130

For they are supported by the guardians of hell
And by all the Compassionate Ones.
So, (behaving) like the subjects of that fiery king,
I should please all sentient beings.

131

Even if such a king were to become angry,
Could he cause the pain of hell,
Which is the fruit I would have to experience
By displeasing sentient beings?

132

And even if such a king were to be kind,
He could not possibly grant me Buddhahood,
Which is the fruit I would obtain
By pleasing sentient beings.

133

Why do I not see
That my future attainment of Buddhahood,
As well as glory, renown and happiness in this very life,
All come from pleasing sentient beings?

134

While in cyclic existence, patience causes
Beauty, health and renown.
Because of these, I shall live for a very long time
And win the extensive pleasure of the universal Chakra Kings.

CHAPTER VII

Enthusiasm

1

Having patience, I should develop enthusiasm;
For Awakening will dwell only in those who exert themselves.
Just as there is no movement without wind,
So merit does not occur without enthusiasm.

2

What is enthusiasm? It is finding joy in what is wholesome.
Its opposing factors are explained
As laziness, attraction to what is harmful
And despising oneself out of despondency.

3

Because of attachment to the pleasurable taste of idleness,
Because of craving for sleep
And because of having no disillusion with the misery of cyclic
    existence,
Laziness grows very strong.

4

Enmeshed in the snare of disturbing conceptions,
I have entered the snare of birth.
Why am I still not aware
That I live in the mouth of the Lord of Death?

5

Do I not see
That he is systematically slaughtering my species?
Whoever remains soundly asleep
(Surely behaves) like a buffalo with a butcher.

6

When having blocked off every (escape) route,
The Lord of Death is looking (for someone to kill),
How can I enjoy eating?
And likewise, how can I enjoy sleep?

7

For as long as death is actually approaching
Then I shall accumulate merits;
Even if I then put a stop to laziness,
What will be the use? That is not the time!

8

When this has not been done, when this is being done
And when this is only half finished,
Suddenly the Lord of Death will come.
And the thought will occur, "Oh no, I am done for!"

9

Their faces flowing with tears
And their eyes red and swollen with sorrow,
My relatives will finally lose hope,
And I shall behold the vision of the messengers of death.

10

Tormented by the memory of my wrongdoing,
And hearing the sounds of hell,
In terror, I shall clothe my body in excrement.
What virtue can I do in such a delirious state?

11

If even in this life I shall be gripped with fear
Like that of a live fish being rolled (in hot sand),
Why even mention the unbearable agonies of hell
That will result from my unwholesome deeds?

12

How can I remain at ease like this,
When I have committed the actions (that will bear fruit)
In my delicate infant's body encountering boiling acids
In the hell of tremendous heat?

13

Much harm befalls those with little forbearance
And those who want results without making any effort.
While clasped by death, they shall cry like the gods,
"Oh no, I am overcome by misery!"

14

Relying upon the boat of a human (body),
Free yourself from the great river of pain!
As it is hard to find this boat again,
This is no time for sleep, you fool.

15

Having rejected the supreme joy of the sacred Dharma,
Which is a boundless source of delight,
Why am I distracted by the causes for pain?
Why do I enjoy frivolous amusements and the like?

16

Without indulging in despondency, I should gather the supports
    (for enthusiasm)
And earnestly take control of myself.
(Then by seeing) the equality between self and others,
I should practice exchanging self for others.

17

I should never indulge in despondency by entertaining such
    thoughts as,
"How shall I ever awaken?"
For the Tathagatas who speak what is true
Have uttered this truth:

18

"If they develop the strength of their exertion,
Even those who are flies, mosquitoes, bees and insects
Will win the unsurpassable Awakening,
Which is so hard to find."[24]

19

(It will be) so, if I do not forsake the Bodhisattvas' way of life.
Why should someone like myself, who has been born in the
    human race,
Not attain Awakening, since I am able to recognize
What is beneficial and what is of harm?

20

-Nevertheless, it frightens me to think
That I may have to give away my arms and legs-
Without discriminating between what is heavy and what is light,
I am reduced to fear through confusion.

21

For over countless myriads of aeons
I have been cut, stabbed, burned,
And flayed alive innumerable times,
But I have not awakened.

22

Yet the suffering
Involved in my awakening will have a limit;
It is like the suffering of having an incision made
In order to remove and destroy greater pain.

23

Even doctors eliminate illness
With unpleasant medical treatments,
So in order to overcome manifold sufferings
I should be able to put up with some discomfort.

24

Yet the Supreme Physician does not employ
Common medical treatments such as these,
With an extremely gentle technique,
He remedies all the greatest ills.

25

At the beginning, the Guide of the World encourages
The giving of such things as food.
Later, when accustomed to this,
One may progressively start to give away even one's flesh.

26

At such a time when my mind is developed
To the point of regarding my body like food,
Then what hardship would there be
When it came to giving away my flesh?

27

Having forsaken all transgression, there would be no suffering,
And due to wisdom, there would be no lack of joy;
But now my mind is afflicted by mistaken conceptions
And my body is caused harm by unwholesome deeds.

28

As their bodies are happy due to their merits,
And their minds are happy due to their wisdom,
Even if they remained in cyclic existence for the sake of others,
Why would the Compassionate Ones ever be upset?

29

Due to the strength of the Awakening Mind,
The Bodhisattvas consume their previous transgressions
And harvests oceans of merit:
Hence they are said to excel the Shravakas.

30

So, having mounted the horse of an Awakening Mind
That dispels all discouragement and weariness,
Who, when they know of this mind that proceeds from joy to joy,
Would ever lapse into despondency?

31

The supports when working for the sake of living beings
Are aspiration,[25] steadfastness, joy and rest.[26]
Aspiration is developed through fear of misery
And by contemplating the benefits of (aspiration) itself.

32

Thus in order to increase my enthusiasm
I should strive to abandon its opposing forces,
To (amass the supports of) aspiration, self-confidence,[27] joy and rest,
To practice in earnest and to become strong in self-control.

33

I shall have to overcome
The boundless faults of myself and others,
And (in order to destroy) each of these faults (alone)
(I may have to strive until) an ocean of aeons is exhausted.

34

Yet if within myself I do not perceive
Even a fraction of the perseverance (required) to exhaust these faults,
Then why do I not have a heart attack?
For now I have become an abode for infinite misery.

35

Likewise, I shall have to realize
Many excellent qualities for myself and others,
And (in order to attain) each of these qualities (alone)
I may have to acquaint myself with its cause until an ocean of
aeons is exhausted.

36

However, I have never developed acquaintance
With even a fraction of these excellences.
How strange it is to squander
This birth I have found by some coincidence.

37

I have not made offerings to the Lord Buddhas,
I have not given the pleasure of great festivals,
I have not performed actions for the teachings,
I have not fulfilled the wishes of the poor,

38

I have not granted fearlessness to the frightened
And I have not given happiness to the weak.
All I have given rise to is
The agonies in the mother's womb, and to suffering.

39

Both now and in previous lives,
Such deprivation has arisen
Because of my lack of aspiring for the Dharma.
Who would ever reject this aspiring for Dharma?

40

The Mighty One himself has said
That aspiration is the root of every facet of virtue;
Its root is constant acquaintance
With the ripening-effects (of actions).

41

(Physical) pain, mental unhappiness,
All the various kinds of fear,
As well as separation from what is desired
All arise from an unwholesome way of life.

42

(However) by committing wholesome actions,
Which are (motivated by aspiration) in the mind,
Wherever I go I shall be presented with
Tokens of the fruit of that merit.

43

Yet by committing negative (actions),
Although I may wish for happiness,
Wherever I go I shall be completely overcome
By weapons of pain (caused) by my wrongful life.

44

As a result of virtue, I shall dwell in the spacious, fragrant and
    cool heart of a lotus flower,
My radiance will be nourished by the food of the Conqueror's
    sweet speech,
My glorious form will spring from a lotus unfolded by the
    Mighty One's light,
And, as a Bodhisattva, I shall abide in the presence of the
    Conquerors.

45

However, as a result of non-virtue, my skin will be ripped off by
    the henchmen of Yama.
In this feeble state, liquid copper melted by tremendous heat will
    be poured into my body.
Pierced by flaming swords and daggers, my flesh will be cut into
    a hundred pieces,
And I shall tumble upon the fiercely blazing iron ground.

46

Therefore, I should aspire for virtue,
And with great respect acquaint myself with it.
Having undertaken the wholesome in the manner of
    Vajradhvaja,[28]
I should then proceed to acquaint myself with self-confidence.

47

First of all, I should examine well what is to be done,
To see whether I can pursue it or cannot undertake it.
(If I am unable,) it is best to leave it,
But once I have started I must not withdraw.

48

(If I do,) then this habit will continue in other lives
And wrongdoing and misery will increase;
Also, other actions done at the time of its fruition
Will be weak and will not be accomplished.

49

Self-confidence should be applied to (wholesome) actions,
The (overcoming) of disturbing conceptions and my ability (to
   do this).
Thinking, "I alone shall do it,"
Is the self-confidence of action.

50

Powerless, their minds disturbed,
People in this world are unable to benefit themselves.
Therefore, I shall do it (for them),
Since unlike me these beings are incapable.

51

(Even) if others are doing inferior tasks,
Why should I sit here (doing nothing)?
I do not do those tasks because of self-importance;
It would be best for me to have no such pride.

52

When crows encounter a dying snake,
They will act as though they were eagles.
(Likewise,) if (my self-confidence) is weak,
I shall be injured by the slightest downfall.

53

How can those who, out of faint-heartedness, have given up
   trying to
Find liberation because of this deficiency?
Yet even the greatest (obstacle) will find it hard to overcome
   (one with a firm mind).

54

Therefore, with a steady mind,
I shall overcome all falls,
For if I am defeated by a fall,
My wish to vanquish the three realms will become a joke.

55

I will conquer everything
And nothing at all shall conquer me!
I, a child of the Lion-like Conqueror,
Should remain self-confident in this way.

56

Whoever has self-importance is destroyed by it,
Is disturbed and has no self-confidence.
For those with self-confidence do not succumb to the power of
   the enemy,
Whereas the former are under the sway of the enemy of self-
   importance.

57

Inflated by the disturbing conception of my self-importance,
I shall be led by it to the lower realms.
It destroys the joyous festival of being human.
I shall become a slave, eating the food of others,

58

Stupid, ugly, feeble and everywhere disrespected.
Tough people bloated by conceit
Are also counted among the self-important;
Tell me, what is more pathetic than this?

59

Whoever seizes self-confidence in order to conquer the enemy
    of self-importance,
They are the self-confident ones, the victorious heroes,
And in addition, whoever definitely conquers the spread of this
    enemy, self-importance,
Completely (wins) the fruit of a Conqueror, fulfilling the wishes
    of the world.

60

If I find myself amidst a crowd of disturbing conceptions,
I shall endure them in a thousand ways;
Like a lion among foxes,
I will not be affected by this disturbing host.

61

Just as men will guard their eyes
When great danger and turmoil occur,
Likewise, I shall never be swayed by the disturbances within my
    mind,
Even at times of great strife.

62

It would be better for me to be burned,
To have my head cut off and to be killed,
Rather then ever bowing down
To those ever-present disturbing conceptions.
(So likewise, in all situations, I should do nothing other than
    what is fit.)29

63

Just like those who yearn for the fruits of play,
(Bodhisattvas) are attracted
To whatever task they may do;
They never have enough, it only brings them joy.

64

Although people work in order to be happy,
It is uncertain whether or not they will find it;
But how can those whose work itself is joy
Find happiness unless they do it?

65

If I feel that I never have enough sensual objects,
Which are like honey smeared upon a razor's edge,
Then why should I ever feel that I have enough
Merit which ripens in happiness and peace?

66

Thus in order to complete this task,
I shall venture into it
Just as an elephant tormented by the mid-day sun
Plunges into a (cool, refreshing) lake.

67

When my strength declines, I should leave whatever I am doing
In order to be able to continue with it later.
Having done something well, I should put it aside
With the wish (to accomplish) what will follow.

68

Just as an old warrior approaches
The swords of an enemy upon the battlefront,
So shall I avoid the weapons of the disturbing conceptions
And skilfully bind this enemy.

69

If someone dropped a sword during a battle,
They would immediately pick it up out of fear.
Likewise, if I lose the weapon of mindfulness,
I should quickly retrieve it, being afraid of hell.

70

Just as poison spreads throughout the body
In dependence upon the (circulation of) blood,

Likewise, if (a disturbing conception) finds an opportunity,
Unwholesomeness will permeate my mind.

71

Those who practice should be as attentive
As a frightened man carrying a jar full of mustard oil,
Who is being threatened by someone with a sword,
(And told) that he will be killed if he spills just one drop.

72

Just as I would swiftly stand up
If a snake came into my lap,
Likewise, if any sleep or laziness occurs,
I shall quickly turn it back.

73

Each time something unwholesome occurs
I should criticize myself,
And then contemplate for a long time
That I shall never let this happen again.

74

"Likewise in all these situations
I shall acquaint myself with mindfulness."
With this (motivation) as a cause, I shall aspire
To meet (with teachers) or accomplish the tasks (they assign me).

75

In order to have strength for everything,
I should recall before undertaking any action
The advice in (the chapter on) conscientiousness,
And then joyfully rise (to the task).

76

Just as the wind blowing back and forth
Controls (the movement of) a piece of cotton,
So shall I be controlled by joy,
And in this way accomplish everything.

Chapter VIII

Meditation

1

Having developed enthusiasm in this way,
I should place my mind in concentration;
For the person whose mind is distracted
Dwells between the fangs of disturbing conceptions.

2

However, through solitude of body and mind
No distractions will occur;
Therefore, I should forsake the worldly life,
And completely discard distorted conceptions.

3

Worldly life is not forsaken because of attachment (to people),
And due to craving for material gain and the like;
Therefore I should entirely forsake these things,
For this is the way in which the wise behave.

4

Having understood that disturbing conceptions are completely
    overcome
By superior insight endowed with calm abiding,
First of all, I should search for calm abiding.
This is achieved through the genuine joy of those unattached to
    worldly life.

5

Because of the obsession one transient being
Has for other transient beings,
They will not see their beloved ones again
For many thousands of lives.

6

Not seeing them, I am unhappy
And my mind cannot be settled in equipoise;
Even if I see them, there is no satisfaction
And, as before, I am tormented by craving.

7

Through being attached to living beings,
I am completely obscured from the perfect reality,
My disillusionment (with cyclic existence) perishes
And, in the end, I am tortured by sorrow.

8

By thinking only of them,
This life will pass without any meaning.
(Furthermore,) impermanent friends and relatives
Will even destroy the Dharma (which leads to) permanent
    (liberation).

9

If I behave in the same way as the childish,
I shall certainly proceed to lower realms,
And if I am led there by those unequal (to the Noble Ones),
What is the use of entrusting myself to the childish?

10

One moment they are friends,
And in the next instant they become enemies.
Since they become angry even in joyful situations,
It is difficult to please ordinary people.

11

They are angry when something of benefit is said,
And they also turn me away from what is beneficial.
If I do not listen to what they say,
They become angry and hence proceed to lower realms.

12

They are envious of superiors, competitive with equals,
Arrogant towards inferiors, conceited when praised,
And if anything unpleasant is said, they become angry.
Never is any benefit derived from the childish.

13

Through associating with the childish,
There will certainly ensue unwholesomeness,
Such as praising myself, belittling others
And discussing the joys of cyclic existence.

14

Devoting myself to others in this way
Will bring about nothing but misfortune,
Because they will not benefit me,
And I shall not benefit them.

15

I should flee far away from childish people.
When they are encountered, though, I should please them by
    being happy.
I should behave well merely out of courtesy,
But not become greatly familiar.

16

In the same way as a bee takes honey from a flower,
I should take merely (what is necessary) for the practice of Dharma,
But remain unfamiliar,
As though I had never seen them before.

17

"I have much material wealth as well as honor,
And many people like me."
Nurturing self-importance in this way
I shall be made terrified after death.

18

So, you thoroughly confused mind,
By the piling up of whatever objects
You are attached to,
Misery a thousandfold will ensue.

19

Hence the wise should not be attached,
(Because) fear is born from attachment.
With a firm mind understand well
That it is the nature of these things to be discarded!

20

Although I may have much material wealth,
Be famous and well-spoken of,
Whatever fame and renown I have amassed
Has no power to accompany me (after death).

21

If there is someone who despises me,
What pleasure can I have in being praised?
And if there is another who praises me,
What displeasure can I have in being despised?

22

If even the Conqueror was unable to please
The various inclinations of different beings,
Then what need to mention a malicious person such as I?
Therefore, I should give up the intention (to associate with) the
worldly.

23

They scorn those who have no material gain
And say bad things about those who do;
How can they, who are by nature so hard to get along with,
Ever derive any pleasure (from me)?

24

It has been said by the Tathagatas
That one should not befriend the childish
Because, unless they get their own way,
These children are never happy.[30]

25

When shall I come to dwell in forests
Amongst the deer, the birds and the trees,
That say nothing unpleasant,
And are delightful to associate with?

26

When dwelling in caves,
In empty shrines and at the feet of trees,
Never look back—
Cultivate detachment.

27

When shall I come to dwell
In places not clung to as "mine",
Which are by nature wide and open,
And where I may behave as I wish, without attachment?

28

When shall I come to live without fear,
Having just a begging bowl and a few odd things,
Wearing clothes not wanted by anyone,
And not even having to hide this body?

29

Having departed to the cemeteries,
When shall I come to understand
That this body of mine and the skeletons of others
Are equal in being subject to decay?

30

Then, because of its odor,
Not even the foxes
Will come close to this body of mine;
For this is what will become of it.

31

Although this body arose as one thing,
The bones and flesh with which it was created
Will break up and separate.
How much more so will friends and others?

32

At birth I was born alone,
And at death, too, I shall die alone;
As this pain cannot be shared by others,
What use are obstacle-making friends?

33

In the same way as travellers on a highway
(Leave one place) and reach (another),
Likewise, those travelling on the path of conditioned existence
(Leave) one birth and reach (another).

34

Until the time comes for this body
To be supported by four pall-bearers
While the worldly (stand around) stricken with grief,
Until then, I shall retire to the forest.

35

Befriending no one and begrudging no one,
My body will dwell alone in solitude.
If I am already counted as a dead man,
When I die there will be no mourners.

36

And as there will be no one around
To disturb me with their mourning,
Thus there will be no one to distract me
From my recollection of the Buddha.

37

Therefore, I shall dwell alone,
Happy and contented with few difficulties,
In very joyful and beautiful forests,
Pacifying all distractions.

38

Having given up all other intentions,
Being motivated by only one thought,
I shall strive to settle my mind in equipoise (by means of calm
    abiding),
And to subdue it (with superior insight).

39

Both in this world and the next,
Desires give rise to great misfortune:
In this life killing, bondage and flaying,
And in the next, the existence of the hells.

40

For the sake of (women), many requests
Are first of all made through go-betweens,
All forms of transgression and even notoriety
Are not avoided for their sake.

41

I engage in fearful deeds for them,
And will even consume my wealth.
But these (very bodies of theirs),
Which I greatly enjoy in the sexual embrace,

42

Are nothing other than skeletons,
They are not autonomous and are identityless.
Rather than being so desirous and completely obsessed,
Why do I not go to the state beyond sorrow (instead)?

43

In the first place, I made efforts to lift (her veil),
And when it was raised she bashfully looked down.
Previously, whether anyone looked or not,
Her face was covered with a cloth.

44

Yet now, why do I run away
Upon directly beholding
This face, which disturbs the mind
As it is being revealed to me by the vultures?

45

(Previously) I completely protected (her body)
When others cast their eyes upon it.
Why, miser, do you not protect it now,
While it is being devoured by these birds?

46

Since vultures and others are eating
This pile of meat that I behold,
Why did I offer flower garlands, sandalwood and ornaments
To that which is now the food of others?

47

If I am frightened by the skeletons I see,
Even though they do not move,
Why am I not frightened by walking corpses
Which are moved around by a few (impulses)?

48

Although I am attached to it when it is covered (with skin),
Why do I not desire it when it is uncovered?
Since I have no need for it then,
Why copulate with it when it is covered?

49

Since both excrement and saliva
Arise solely from food,
Why do I dislike excrement,
And find joy in saliva?

50

Cotton, too, is soft to the touch,
But while I find no (sexual) delight in a pillow,
I think that (a woman's body) does not emit a putrid odor.
Lustful One, you are confused as to what is unclean!

51

Thinking that they cannot sleep with this cotton,
Although it is soft to the touch,
Confused, negative and lustful people
Become angry towards it (instead).

52

If I am not attached to what is unclean,
Then why do I copulate with the lower parts of others' bodies,
Which are merely cages of bones tied together with muscles,
Plastered over with the mud of flesh?

53

I myself contain many unclean things
Which I constantly have to experience;
So why, because of an obsession for uncleanliness,
Do I desire other bags of filth?

54

-But it is the flesh that I enjoy-
If this is what I wish to touch and behold,
Why do I not desire it in its natural state,
Devoid of any mind?

55

Furthermore, any mind that I may desire
Is unable to be touched or beheld,
And whatever I am able to touch will not be mental;
So why indulge in this meaningless copulation?

56

It is not so strange that I do not understand
The bodies of others to be of an unclean nature,
But it is indeed strange that I do not understand
My very own body to be by nature unclean.

57

Having forsaken the young lotus flower
Unfolded by beams of sunlight free from cloud,
Why, with a mind craving for what is unclean,
Do I revel in a cage of filth?

58

Since I do not wish to touch
A place that is smeared with excrement,
Then why do I wish to touch the body
From which that (excrement) arose?

59

If I am not attached to what is unclean,
Why do I copulate with the lower parts of others' bodies,
Which arise from the unclean field (of a womb)
And are produced by the seeds within it?

60

I have no wish for a small, dirty maggot
Which has come from a pile of filth,
So why do I desire this body, which by nature is grossly unclean,
For it too was produced by filth?

61

Not only do I not disparage
The uncleanliness of my own body,
But, because of an obsession for what is unclean,
I desire other bags of filth as well.

62

Even attractive things such as savory foods,
Cooked rice and vegetables,
Make the ground dirty and unclean,
Should they be spat out after being in the mouth.

63

Although such uncleanliness is obvious,
If I still have doubts I should go to the cemeteries
And look at the unclean bodies (of others)
That have been thrown away there.

64

Having realized that, when their skin is rent open,
They give rise to a great deal of fear,
How will such things as these
Ever again give rise to joy?

65

The scents with which someone's body is anointed
Are sandalwood and the like, but not that of the other's body.
So why am I attached to others' (bodies)
Because of scents that are other (than theirs)?

66

Since the body has a naturally foul odor,
Isn't it good to be unattached to it?
Why do those who crave for the meaningless things of the world
Anoint this body with pleasant scents?

67

And furthermore, if it is the pleasant scent of sandalwood,
How can it come from the body?
So why am I attached to others' (bodies)
Because of scents that are other (than theirs)?

68

Since the naked body, (left) in its natural state,
Is very frightening due to its long hair and nails,
Its yellowish foul-smelling teeth
And its being coated with the odor of dirt,

69

Why do I make such an effort to polish it,
Like (cleaning) a weapon that will cause me harm?
Hence this entire world is disturbed with insanity,
Due to the exertions of those who are confused about themselves.

70

When my mind rises (above worldly concerns),
Through having beheld nothing but skeletons in the cemetery,
Will there be any joy in graveyard cities
Which are filled with moving skeletons?

71

Furthermore, these unclean (female bodies)
Are not found without paying a price.
In order to obtain them, I exhaust myself
And (in future) will be injured in the hells.

72

As a child, I am unable to increase my wealth,
And as a youth, what can I do (being unable to afford a wife)?
At the end of my life, when I have the wealth,
Being an old man, what good will sex be then?

73

Some malicious and lustful people
Wear themselves out by working all day
And, when they return home (in the evening),
Their exhausted bodies lie prostrate like corpses.

74

Some have the suffering of being disturbed with travel
And having to go a long way from home.
Although they long for their spouses,
They do not see them for years at a time.

75

And some who wish for benefit
Due to confusion, even sell themselves for the sake of (women
    and the like):
But not attaining what they wish,
They are aimlessly driven by the winds of others' actions.

76

Some sell their own bodies
And, without any power, are employed by others.
Even when their wives give birth,
Their children fall at the feet of trees and in lonely places.

77

Some fools who are deceived by desire and,
Wishing for a livelihood, think, "I shall earn my living (as a
    soldier);"
Then, although afraid of losing their lives, they go to war.
Others become slaves for the sake of profit.

78

Some lustful people even cut their bodies,
Others impale themselves on the points of sticks,
Some stab themselves with daggers,
And others burn themselves—such things as these are quite
apparent.

79

Due to the torment involved in collecting it, protecting and
finally losing it,
I should realize wealth to be fraught with infinite problems.
Those who are distracted by their attachment to it
Have no opportunity to gain freedom from the misery of condi-
tioned existence.

80

In the same way as animals drawing carriages
Are only able to eat a few mouthfuls of grass,
Likewise, desirous people
Have many disadvantages such as these, and little (profit),

81

And since even animals can obtain this (little profit),
Those who are pained by their (previous) actions
Waste these leisures and endowments, so difficult to find,
For the sake of something trivial that is not so scarce.

82

The objects of desire will certainly perish,
And then I shall fall into hellish states.
However, Buddhahood itself is attained
With just one millionth of the difficulty

83

Involved in continually exhausting myself
For the sake of what is not very great.
(Hence) the desirous experience greater misery than (those fol-
lowing) the Awakening way of life—
But (for them) there is no Awakening.

84

When one has contemplated the miseries of hell,
(It will be clear that) there is nothing comparable
To the harm caused to desirous beings,
Even by weapons, poison, fire, ravines and foes.

85

Having in this way developed disillusionment with desire,
I should generate joy for solitude.
The fortunate ones stroll in peaceful forests,
Devoid of disputes and disturbing conceptions.

86

(They live) in joyful houses of vast flat stones,
Cooled by the sandal-scented moonlight,
Fanned by the peaceful, silent forest breeze,
Thinking of what is of benefit for others.

87

They dwell for as long as they wish
In empty houses, at the feet of trees and in caves.
Having abandoned the pain of clinging to and guarding (posses-
    sions),
They abide independent, free of care,

88

Living as they choose, desireless,
Having no ties with anyone—
Even the powerful have difficulty finding
A life as happy and content as this.

89

Having in such ways as these
Thought about the excellences of solitude,
I should completely pacify distorted conceptions
And meditate on the Awakening Mind.

90

First of all, I should make an effort
To meditate upon the equality between self and others.
I should protect all beings as I do myself
Because we are all equal in (wanting) pleasure and (not wanting)
pain.

91

Although there are many different parts and aspects such as the
hand,
As a body that is to be protected, they are one.
Likewise, all the different sentient beings, in their pleasure and
their pain,
Have a wish to be happy that is the same as mine.

92

The suffering that I experience
Does not cause any harm to others.
But that suffering (is mine) because of my conceiving of (myself
as) "I";
Thereby it becomes unbearable.

93

Likewise, the misery of others
Does not befall me.
Nevertheless, by conceiving of (others as) "I," their suffering
becomes mine;
Therefore, it too should be hard to bear.

94

Hence I should dispel the misery of others
Because it is suffering, just like my own,
And I should benefit others
Because they are sentient beings, just like myself.

95

When both myself and others
Are similar in that we wish to be happy,
What is so special about me?
Why do I strive for my happiness alone?

96

And when both myself and others
Are similar in that we do not wish to suffer,
What is so special about me?
Why do I protect myself and not others?

97

-Why should I protect them,
If their suffering does not cause me any harm?-
Then why protect myself against future suffering,
If it causes me no harm now?

98

It is a mistaken conception to think
That I shall experience (the suffering of my next life).
For it is another person who dies,
And another that will be reborn.

99

-Surely whenever there is suffering
The (sufferers) must protect themselves from it-
Yet the suffering of the foot is not that of the hand,
Why then does one protect the other?

100

-Although this may not be justified,
It is done because of grasping at a self-
Yet surely whatever is not justified for myself or others
Should at all costs be rejected.

101

Such things as a continuum and an aggregation
Are false in the same way as prayer beads and an army.
There is no (real) owner of suffering,
Therefore who has control over it?

102

There being no (inherent) owner of suffering,
There can be no distinction at all between (that of myself and others).
Thus I shall dispel it because it hurts.
Why am I so certain (that I shouldn't eliminate the suffering of
    others)?

103

-But (since neither the suffering nor the sufferer truly exist), why
    should I turn away the misery of all?-
This is no ground for argument,
For if I prevent my own (sufferings), surely I should prevent the
    (sufferings) of all.
If not, since I am just like (other) sentient beings, (I should not
    prevent my own suffering, either).

104

-Since this compassion will bring me much misery,
Why should I exert myself to develop it?-
Should I contemplate the suffering of living creatures,
How could the misery of compassion be more?

105

If, by one person's suffering,
The suffering of many would be destroyed,
Surely kindhearted people would accept it
For the sake of themselves and others?

106

Thus the Bodhisattva Supushpa chandra,
Although aware of the harm the king would cause him,

Accepted his own suffering
In order to eradicate the miseries of many.[31]

107

Thus, because they love to pacify the pains of others,
Those whose minds are attuned in this way
Would enter even the deepest hell
Just as a wild goose plunges into a lotus pool.

108

Will not the ocean of joy
That shall exist when all beings are free
Be sufficient for me?
What am I doing wishing for my liberation alone?

109

Therefore, although working for the benefit of others,
I should not be conceited or (consider myself) wonderful.
And because of the joy there is in solely doing this,
I should have no hope for any ripening-effect.

110

Therefore, just as I protect myself
From unpleasant things however small,
In the same way I should act towards others
With a compassionate and caring mind.

111

Although the basis is quite impersonal,
Through (constant) familiarity
I have come to regard
The drops of sperm and blood of others as "I".

112

So in the same way, why should I be unable
To regard the bodies of others as "I"?
Hence it is not difficult to see
That my body is also that of others.

113

Having seen the mistakes in (cherishing) myself
And the ocean of good in (cherishing) others,
I shall completely reject all selfishness
And accustom myself to accepting others.

114

In the same way as the hands and so forth
Are regarded as limbs of the body,
Likewise, why are embodied creatures
Not regarded as limbs of life?

115

Through acquaintance has the thought of "I" arisen
Towards this impersonal body;
So in a similar way, why should it not arise
Towards other living beings?

116

When I work in this way for the sake of others,
I should not let conceit or (the feeling that I am) wonderful arise.
It is just like feeding myself-
I hope for nothing in return.

117

Therefore, just as I protect myself
From unpleasant things, however slight,
In the same way, I should habituate myself
To have a compassionate and caring mind towards others.

118

It is out of his great compassion
That the Lord Avalokiteshvara has (even) blessed his name
To dispel the nervousness
Of being among other people.[32]

119

I should not turn away from what is difficult;
For by the power of familiarity,
I may be made unhappy even when someone
Whose name once frightened me is not around.

120

Thus whoever wishes to quickly afford protection
To both the self and other beings
Should practice that holy secret:
The exchanging of self for others.

121

Because of attachment to my body,
Even a small object of fear frightens me.
So who would not revile, as an enemy,
This body that gives rise to fear?

122

By wishing for a means to remedy
The hunger, thirst and sickness of the body,
I might kill birds, fish and deer
And loiter by the sides of roads (to rob others).

123

If, for the sake of its profit and comfort,
I would kill even my father and mother,
And steal the property of the Triple Gem,
Then I would undoubtedly proceed to burn in the flames of the
    deepest hell.

124

Therefore what adept would desire,
Protect and venerate this body?
Who would not scorn it
And regard it as an enemy?

125

"If I give this, what shall I (have left to) enjoy?"-
Such selfish thinking is the way of ghosts;
"If I enjoy this, what shall I (have left to) give?"-
Such selfless thinking is a quality of the gods.

126

If, for my own sake, I cause harm to others,
I shall be tormented in hellish realms;
But if, for the sake of others, I cause harm to myself,
I shall acquire all that is magnificent.

127

By holding myself in high esteem
I shall find myself in unpleasant realms, ugly and stupid;
But should this (attitude) be shifted to others,
I shall acquire honors in a joyful realm.

128

If I employ others for my own purposes,
I myself shall experience servitude;
But if I use myself for the sake of others,
I shall experience only lordliness.

129

Whatever joy there is in this world
All comes from desiring others to be happy,
And whatever suffering there is in this world
All comes from desiring myself to be happy.

130

What need is there to say much more?
The childish work for their own benefit,
The Buddhas work for the benefit of others.
Just look at the difference between them!

131

If I do not actually exchange my happiness
For the sufferings of others,
I shall not attain the state of Buddhahood
And even in cyclic existence shall have no joy.

132

Let alone what is beyond this world.
Because my servants do no work
And because my masters give me no pay,
Even the needs of this life will not be fulfilled.

133

(By rejecting the method that) establishes both foreseeable and
    unforeseeable joy,
I cast magnificent delight completely aside
And then, because of inflicting misery on others,
In confusion I seize hold of unbearable pain.

134

If all the injury,
Fear and pain in this world
Arise from grasping at a self,
Then what use is that great ghost to me?

135

If I do not completely forsake it
I shall be unable to put an end to suffering,
Just as I cannot avoid being burned
If I do not cast aside the fire (I hold).

136

Therefore, in order to allay the harms inflicted upon me
And in order to pacify the sufferings of others,
I shall give myself up to others
And cherish them as I do my very self.

137

"I am under the control of others,"
Of this, mind, you must be certain;
Now, except for benefitting every creature,
You must not think of anything else.

138

For my sake, I should not do anything
With these eyes and so forth, which I have left at the disposal of
      others.
It is quite incorrect to do anything with them
Which is contrary to the benefit (of others).

139

Thus sentient beings should be my main (concern).
Whatever I behold upon my body
I should rob and use
For the benefit of others.

140

Considering lesser beings and so forth as myself,
And considering myself as the other,
(In the following way) I should meditate upon envy, competi-
      tiveness and self-importance,
With a mind free of distorted concepts:[33]

141

"He is honored, but I am not;
I have not found wealth such as he.
He is praised, but I am despised;
He is happy, but I suffer.

142

"I have to do all the work,
While he remains comfortably at rest.
He is renowned as great in this world, but I as inferior,
With no good qualities at all.

143

"But what do you mean I have no good qualities?
I have all good qualities.
Compared to many, he is inferior,
And compared to many, I am high.

144

"The deteriorated state of my morals and views
Is not due to me, but due to my disturbing conceptions,
In whatever way he is able, he should heal me,
Willingly I shall accept any discomfort involved.

145

"But I am not being healed by him,
So why does he belittle me?
What use are his good qualities to me?
(Although) he has good qualities, (he does not benefit me)

146

"With no compassion for the beings
Who dwell in the poisonous mouth of harmful realms,
Externally he is proud of his good qualities
And wishes to put down the wise.

147

"In order that I may excel
He who is regarded as equal with me,
I shall definitely strive to attain material gain and honor for myself,
Even (by such means as) verbal dispute.

148

"By all means, I shall make clear to the entire world
All the good qualities I have,
But I shall not let anyone hear
Of any good qualities he may have.

149

"Also I shall hide all my faults;
I will be venerated, but not he;
I will find a great deal of material gain;
I will be honored, but he shall not.

150

"For a long time I shall look with pleasure
At his being made inferior;
He will become the laughing-stock of all,
Regarded among everyone as an object of scorn and derision.

151

"It is said that this deluded one
Is trying to compete with me,
But how can he be equal with me
In learning, intelligence, form, class or wealth?

152

"Thus, upon hearing of my good qualities
That have been made well-known to all,
I shall thoroughly enjoy the satisfaction
Of the pleasant, tingling sensation that occurs.

153

"Even though he has some possessions,
If he is working for me,
I shall give him just enough to live on,
And by force I'll take (the rest).

154

"His happiness and comfort will decline
And I shall always cause him harm,
For hundreds of times in this cycle of rebirth
He has caused harm to me."

155

Because of desiring to benefit yourself, O mind,
All weariness you have gone through
Over countless past aeons
Has only succeeded in achieving misery.

156

Therefore, I shall definitely engage myself
In working for the benefit of others,
For since the words of the Mighty One are infallible,
I shall behold its advantages in the future.

157

If, in the past, I had practiced
This act (of exchanging self for others),
A situation such as this, devoid of the magnificence and bliss of a
    Buddha,
Could not possibly have come about.

158

Therefore, just as I have come to hold as "I"
These drops of sperm and blood of others,
Likewise, through acquaintance
I should also come to regard all others.

159

Having thoroughly examined myself (to see
Whether I am really working for) others (or not),
I shall steal whatever appears on my body and use it for the
    benefit of others.

160

"I am happy but others are sad,
I am high though others are low,
I benefit myself but not others."
Why am I not envious of myself?

161

I must separate myself from happiness
And take upon myself the sufferings of others.
"Why am I doing this now?"
In this way, I should examine myself for faults.

162

Although others may do something wrong,
I should transform it into a fault of my own;
But should I do something even slightly wrong,
I shall openly admit it to many people.

163

By further describing the renown of others,
I should make it outshine my own.
Just like the lowest kind of servant,
I should employ myself for the benefit of all.

164

I should not praise my naturally fault-ridden self
For some temporary good quality it may have,
I shall never let even a few people know
Of any good qualities I may possess.

165

In brief, for the sake of living creatures,
May all the harms
I have selfishly caused to others
Descend upon me myself.

166

I should not be dominating and aggressive,
Acting in a self-righteous, arrogant way;
Instead, like a newly married bride,
I should be bashful, timid and restrained.

167

Thus, O mind, you should (think) and abide in this way
And not act (selfishly) as (before).
If, under the control (of self-cherishing) you transgress (this code),
Your (selfishness) will be your end.

168

However, mind, although you have been advised,
If you do not act in a like manner,
Then since all misfortunes will entrust themselves to you,
You will only be destined to destruction.

169

That previous time when you could overcome me
Is now past;
Now I see (your nature and your faults),
And wherever you go I shall destroy your arrogance.

170

I should immediately cast aside all thoughts
Of working for my own sake.
By having sold you to others,
I shall not become discouraged, but shall offer up all your
    strength (to others).

171

If, having become unconscientious,
I do not give you to all living beings,
It is certain that you will deliver me
To the guardians of the hells.

172

For ages have you dealt with me like this
And I have suffered long;
But now, recalling all my grudges,
I shall overcome your selfish thoughts.

173

Likewise, if I wish to be happy,
I should not be happy with myself;
And similarly, if I wish to be protected
I should constantly protect all others.

174

To whatever degree
I take great care of this body,
To that degree, I shall fall
Into a state of extreme helplessness.

175

Having fallen in this way, if my desires
Are unable to be fulfilled
Even by everything upon this earth,
What else will be able to satisfy them?

176

(Being) unable (to fulfill them, though) desiring (to do so),
Disturbing conceptions and a dissatisfied mind will ensue.
However, if I do not depend on any (material) things,
The exhaustion of my good fortune will be unknown.

177

Therefore, I shall never create an opportunity
For the desires of the body to increase.
For whatever I do not grasp as attractive,
These are the best of all possessions.

178

In the end (my body) will turn to dust;
Unable to move (by itself), it will be propelled by other (forces).
Why do I grasp this unbearable
And unclean form as "I"?

179

Whether it lives or whether it dies,
What use is this machine to me?
How is it different from a clod of earth?
O why do I not dispel this pride (of it being "I" and "mine")!

180

Having accumulated suffering for no purpose
Because of my honoring and serving this body,
What use is attachment and anger
For this thing that is similar to a piece of wood?

181

Whether I am caring for my body in this way,
Or whether it is being eaten by vultures,
It has no attachment or hatred towards these things—
Why then am I so attached to it?

182

If (my body) knows no anger when derided
And no pleasure when praised,
For what reason
Am I wearing myself out like this?

183

-Yet I want this body of mine,
Both it and I are friends-
Since all beings want their bodies,
Why do I not find joy in theirs?

184

Therefore, in order to benefit all beings
I shall give up this body without any attachment.
Although it may have many faults,
I should look after it while experiencing (the results of my
     previous) actions.

185

So enough of this childish behavior!
I shall follow in the steps of the wise,
And having recalled the advice concerning conscientiousness,
I shall turn away sleep and mental dullness.

186

Just like the compassionate Children of the Conqueror,
I shall patiently accept what I have to do;
For if I do not make a constant effort day and night,
When will my misery ever come to an end?

187

Therefore, in order to dispel the obscurations,
I shall withdraw my mind from mistaken ways
And constantly place it in equipoise
Upon the perfect object.

CHAPTER IX

Wisdom

(For the sake of clarity, the entire ninth chapter—with the exception of the introductory and concluding verses—will be presented in the prose form of a dialogue. The dialogue takes place between the Madhyamika school,[34] represented by the author Shantideva, and various other Buddhist and non-Buddhist schools. A brief explanation of the tenets of the different schools will be given as they are introduced. The root text of the author is indicated by the passages in italics. All the additional material, including the outline, is drawn from the commentary of Thog-me Zang-po. The entire outline in the form of an index can be found appended to this text. The numbers in brackets indicate the individual stanzas of the root text.)

(1) *All of these practices were taught*
By the Mighty One for the sake of wisdom.
Therefore, those who wish to pacify suffering
Should generate this wisdom.

I. RECOGNITION OF THE NATURE OF WISDOM

A. ASCERTAINING THE TWO TRUTHS

(2) Deceptive truths, so called because they are truths established from the point of view of deceived minds that obscure the real meaning, and *ultimate truths*, so called because they are truths comprehended by a Superior's wisdom to which no (deceptive truths) appear, *are accepted as the two truths. Ultimate* truths *are not objects experienced by the mind*; but *here "the mind"* is to be understood as the *deceptive* (mind) that obscures one from seeing ultimate truths.

(3) *Two types of person are seen* to experience *these* two truths: *yogis* endowed with the concentration of superior insight and calm

abiding, *and common people* who are not so endowed. *Common people* consider the body to be a unit, the mind to be permanent and so forth. *Yogis*, however, contradict (these views) with reasonings such as: "The body is not a unit because it has many parts," and "The mind is not permanent because it changes into something else." (4) *Furthermore, among the yogis*, i.e. the Proponents of External Existence,[35] the Chittamatrins[36] and the Madhyamikas, there are *differences* in their *understanding* of the nature of knowable entities. Thereby those with *the higher views* progressively *contradict* those with *lower views. With examples* such as the magicians's illusion, which are *accepted* as unreal *by both* yogis and common people, it is proven to the Proponents of External Existence that, although something may appear to their minds, it does not have to be real. Thus if the minds of (these yogis) can be established as deceptive, it goes without saying that the same can be established about the minds of the common people.

1. Refuting Objections Concerning Deceptive Truths

Question: If all phenomena were not truly existent, there would be no attainment of Awakening from the practices of giving and so forth.[37] Therefore, what reason would there be to practice them for that purpose?

Answer: Although phenomena do not exist ultimately (i.e. truly), *because, unanalyzed*, they do exist deceptively, it is not contradictory to engage in the practices of giving and so forth *for the sake of* obtaining *the fruit* of Awakening.

Question: Since phenomena appear to both yogis and common people, why should there be a dispute over them?

Answer: (5) Although they are similar in appearance, *common people behold* forms and other such *things and conceive of them to be really existent*; they do *not* understand them to be *like an illusion*. However, since yogis do understand them to exist in such a way, it is *here* that *the yogis and the common people disagree*.

Question: Since (6) *forms and so forth* are established by *true perception*,[38] isn't it contradictory to say that they are false?

Answer: There is no contradiction, because *such* things *are* merely worldly *conventions, but* they are not true *for a valid cognition* (of an ultimate truth). *This is just like the unclean* body *being known deceptively as clean.* In fact, *such* a cognition is *false.*

Question: If all phenomena have no (true) nature, why did the Buddha say that things have a momentarily impermanent nature?

Answer: Such statements have to be interpreted. Having in mind their mere apparent nature, (7) *the Protector Buddha taught things to be impermanent for the sake of* progressively *guiding ordinary people* who conceive of true existence (towards a correct understanding). *However, in actuality such* things *are not* truly *momentary.*

Question: Yet because this momentary nature does not appear to ordinary people, *is it not a contradiction* to say it *even* exists *deceptively?*

Answer: Although it does not appear to the common person, because it appears to those (8) *yogis* who have merely seen personal identitylessness, there is *no mistake* in its being a *deceptive* truth.

Question: Doesn't this contradict the statement that to see the momentary (nature of things) is to see Truth itself?

Answer: *Compared to the worldly* view of things as permanent and so forth, the yogi's vision of momentariness is posited as *a vision of Reality* itself. *Otherwise,* if in comparison to the yogis, the common people saw Reality, then *the yogi's definite understanding of the uncleanliness of a woman's body would be contradicted by the worldly person's* apprehension of it as clean.

Question: If all phenomena were not truly existent, then since the Buddha, too, would be false, would no merits occur from worshipping him?

Answer: (9) *In the same way* that, for you, truly existent merits occur from worshipping *a truly existent* Conqueror, *similarly,* for us, illusion-like *merits* are obtained *from* venerating *an illusion-like Conqueror.*

Question: Yet if sentient beings were like an illusion, then after they die, how would they be reborn?

Answer: (10) *For as long as the necessary conditions are assembled, for that long even illusions will occur.* Although they are unreal, they are similar to sentient beings in the fact that they arise from conditions. *Why, merely by their longer duration, should sentient beings be more real* than illusions? Then it would follow that illusions that last a long time are more real than those that last a short time.

Question: Nevertheless, if this were the case, would not the killing of a sentient being by another sentient being and the killing of an illusory person by another illusory person be equivalent transgressions? And would not charity between sentient beings and charity between illusory people be equivalent virtues?

Answer: (11) *Because an illusory person* who kills or gives something to another illusory person *has no mind, no transgression* or virtue *accrues* from his actions. Whereas if such actions are committed by a sentient being *endowed with an illusion-like mind,* since the agent has a mind which can love and hate, *merits* and *transgressions do accrue* from that agent's actions. (12) *Because the mantras and so forth* that cause illusions *do not have the ability* to produce minds, *illusory minds are not produced* from them, whereas the causes for sentient beings do have the ability to produce minds. Although false, the different (illusions that) result depend upon different causes; in this way, *the illusions that arise from a variety of different conditions also vary.* They are produced from different causes, but (13) *nowhere is there one condition which has the ability* to produce all the effects.

Question: *If, ultimately,* all sentient beings are by nature in *the state beyond sorrow* (i.e. Nirvana)[39] although *deceptively* they are in *cyclic existence*, then for the same reason, (14) *since*, in terms of appearance, *the Buddha would be in cyclic existence, what would be the use of the Bodhisattva's way of life?*

Answer: *If their conditions are not discontinued, even* illusions *will not cease to be.* Likewise, since sentient beings have not discontinued the conditions for cyclic existence, they are in cyclic existence, but (15) *since the Buddha has discontinued these conditions, even deceptively he does not exist* with the nature of one in cyclic existence.

2. Refuting the Objections of the Chittamatrins Concerning Ultimate Truths

(The Chittamatrins are the followers of the idealist "Mind-Only" school of Mahayana Buddhism who maintain that no external objects exist. For them, the mind is not conditioned by an object of a different nature than itself, rather the mind and its object are one in nature and the only nominally distinct. The mind is regarded as truly existent, whereas external objects are denied. To establish the true existence of consciousness they posit self-cognition, a non-deceived aspect of mind that has the function of being conscious of only consciousness itself.)

Chittamatrin: *If no deceived* consciousnesses *exist*, then *what* (mind) can *refer to the illusion-like appearances?*

Madhyamika: (16) *If illusion-like (external) objects are not real for you, what can be referred* to?

Chittamatrin: *Although* (external) objects *do not really exist*, consciousness does *truly exist.* Therefore, since *the images* (of objects) which appear (to consciousness) *are the mind itself*, they are suitable to be referred to (by consciousness).

Madhyamika: (17) *If the mind itself and the illusion-like objects are one substance, then*, since there would be no beholder and no beheld, *what* (object) *would be beheld by what* (mind)? *It has been said by the Protector of the World himself that the mind does not have the ability to behold the mind.* (18) *Just as the blade of a sword cannot cut itself, likewise the mind cannot behold itself.*[40]

Chittamatrin: *Just as a light completely illuminates* itself, so does the mind know itself.

Madhyamika: (19) *The light does not illuminate* itself, *because* something that is to be illuminated has to first of all be unilluminated, but as soon as the light is lit *it is never obscured by any darkness* (i.e. unilluminated).

Chittamatrin: Take for example two kinds of blueness: blueness that appears in dependence *upon another* blue colored object, *like the blue* reflected *in* a clear piece of *glass*, and blueness that does *not* appear *in dependence upon something else*, like the natural color of blue in lapis lazuli. (20) *Likewise, some* objects such as jugs *depend upon other* things such as lights that illuminate them and consciousnesses that know them, *whereas such* things as lights and feelings of pleasure and pain *are beheld without* any such *dependence*.

Madhyamika: This is not so because, since the blueness of lapis lazuli is established as blueness as soon as it comes into being, *it is not something which, previously having not been blue, makes itself blue.* Therefore, this example is unsuitable to illustrate self-illumination and self-cognition.[41] Conventionally, (21) *upon being perceived by consciousness, it can be said that a light illuminates itself,* but ultimately, *upon being perceived by what can it be said that the mind illuminates* itself? Thus the example and what it illustrates are not comparable. Since ultimately neither self-cognition nor other-cognition are established (as truly existent), (22) *no mind at all can behold* (a truly existent consciousness). Thus *it is meaningless to discuss* whether *such* a mind has the quality of *illuminating itself or not.* This would be *like* discussing whether *the looks of the daughter of a barren woman* are attractive or not.

Chittamatrin: (23) *If self-cognition did not exist, how would we able to have a memory of consciousness?* Since we could have no such memory, the existence of self-cognition is established by the reason of (its being a necessary factor in the process of the recollection of consciousness).

Madhyamika: There is no certainty of this; without (the consciousness) experiencing itself, *it is remembered from its relationship to the experiencing of other* objects such as forms. For example, although the (hibernating) bear does not experience being *poisoned* (when bitten) *by a rat*, later, from hearing the sound of thunder (in spring time, he awakens and) experiences pain. From this he indirectly remembers (that he must have been poisoned. The means whereby consciousness is recalled is) *similar* (to this).

Chittamatrin: (24) *If someone with the necessary causal conditions* such as concentration *can see* the consciousnesses of others from afar, *therefore* it must be possible to *clearly* behold *one's own consciousness* which is so near.

Madhyamika: This is not necessarily so, because although *from application of an eye-lotion* (consecrated by) *powerful attainments*, *treasure vases can be seen* far beneath the earth, *the eye-lotion itself*, which is much closer, *cannot* be seen.

Chittamatrin: If self-cognition were non-existent, other-cognitions would also be non-existent.[42] Therefore, there would be no such thing as seeing, hearing and so forth.

Madhyamika: (25) The mere appearances of *seeing, hearing and perceiving are not being negated* here. *It is the conception of them as truly existent that is to be reversed*, since *this is the cause for suffering*.

Chittamatrin: (26) *These illusion*-like objects *are not* external objects *other than the mind*, yet *although not other*, they *cannot be considered* as being the mind itself. Thus they are phenomena which are indescribably other than the mind.

Madhyamika: *If something is a thing, how can it be neither the* mind *nor other* than it? It has to be one or the other; but *if you say that it is neither* one nor *the* other, then *it would not be a thing* because such a thing could not possibly exist.

(27) *Just as* in the Chittamatra system *illusion*-like *objects are not truly existent but can still be seen*, *similarly*, although the mind is not truly existent, conventionally it can appear as the beholder.

Chittamatrin: *Cyclic existence,* (the state in which subject and object) appear as two (substantially distinct things), *has as the basis* of its deceptive appearance *something real,* namely a truly existent, non-dual consciousness.[43] *Otherwise, if it did not have something real as its basis, it would be just like space* and would not (be a state which) could appear as real subjects and objects.

Madhyamika: (28) *If* the dualistic state of cyclic existence *depended upon* something real, *how could it have the function of* appearing as real subjects and objects? It would follow that it could not because *real,* (truly existent) *things do not exist.* Thus in your tradition, whatever is *mind would become a solitary* non-dual consciousness *unassisted* by any object.[44] (29) *If* it were true that, in this way, *the mind existed separately from its objects, then all* sentient beings *would become Tathagatas.* Therefore, *what* advantage *is there in considering* the basis of cyclic existence *to be merely mind?*

B. Establishing as the Path the Knowledge that Deceptive Truths are Like Illusions

Question: (30) *Even if one knows* that all phenomena *are like an illusion, how will disturbing conceptions be turned away?* For instance, a magician *who creates an* illusory *woman can still have desire for her.*

Answer: (31) *The creator* of this illusion *has not abandoned the tendencies of the disturbing conception* of desire *towards knowable entities* such as women. *Therefore, when he sees the* illusory woman, *the tendency* (to see her) *emptiness is* very *weak.* Although the illusion may be understood to be empty (of being a real woman), through not understanding phenomena to be empty (of true existence), the tendencies of desire are aroused.

(32) *However, through developing the tendency* to know all phenomena *as empty, the tendency* of apprehending *things* as truly existent *will be abandoned.* And *through familiarizing* oneself *with the fact that no phenomena*—emptinesses as well as (deceptive truths)—are established (as truly existent), *in the future* the

apprehension of emptiness as well as false phenomena (as being truly existent) *will be abandoned*. At this time, it will be impossible for any disturbing conceptions to occur.

(33) *When it is said that no thing exists*, this means that *the thing* to be negated (true existence), *which is under examination*, is *not to be apprehended. At that time, since* (true existence), *the basis* in dependence upon which *no* true *existence* is posited, *is removed, how can* non-true existence *remain before the mind* as truly existent? Just as the son of a barren woman does not exist, neither does his *dying*. (34) *Once neither a thing nor a non-thing* (its emptiness) *remains before the mind, then as there is no other* alternative, such as something being both a thing and a non-thing, or being neither a thing nor a non-thing, finally the mind *that apprehends* (truly existent) objects *will cease and be totally pacified*.

Question: If this were the case, then because he would not reflect, "I shall do this," how could the Buddha act for the benefit of others?

Answer: (35) *Wish-fulfilling trees and wish-granting gems*, although they have no conceptual motivations, *completely fulfill hopes* because of their own power and the merits accumulated by people. *Likewise, through the force* of both the purity *of the disciples'* minds *and the prayers* a Buddha makes to work for their welfare while existing as a Bodhisattva, the physical *body of a Conqueror appears* and benefit is forthcoming.

Question: Since the prayers of the Bodhisattvas cease upon attaining Buddhahood, wouldn't it be impossible for them to have any effect at that time?

Answer: (36) *For example, although* the Brahmin Sanku *passed away a long time ago, the Garuda Reliquary which he consecrated* with the force of his mantra *is still able to neutralize poisons*. (37) *Similarly, the reliquary of a Conqueror's body is formed in accordance with the actions* and prayers when (the Conqueror) was a Bodhisattva. *Although the Bodhisattva has now passed beyond sorrow* into the non-abiding Nirvana, and that conceptual desire to accomplish the welfare of others has ceased, *the Conqueror still accomplishes all that is of benefit for them*.

Shravaka: (38) *If* the Buddha has no (conceptual) *mind, can* meritorious *fruits occur from worshipping him?*

Madhyamika: There is no fault, *because it has been explained that* the merits from worshipping the Buddha *while he was alive and* from worshipping his relics *when he has passed beyond sorrow are exactly the same.* (39) *It is established through scriptural authority that fruits occur* both from worshipping a Buddha who has no conceptual mind as well as from a Buddha who (is considered) *deceptively* to have a conceptual mind and *ultimately* to be truly existent. *For example, just as* you accept that a truly existent fruit of merit occurs *from* worshipping *a truly existent Buddha* endowed with a mind, we, too, accept that false (non-truly existent) merits occur from worshipping a false (non-truly existent) Buddha.

C. ESTABLISHING AS THE PATH THE KNOWLEDGE THAT ULTIMATE TRUTHS ARE EMPTINESSES

Vaibashika: (40) *Through* cultivating a direct *vision of* the aspects of the Four (Noble) *Truths,* such as impermanence and so forth, *one will be liberated from* disturbing conceptions: *so what is the point of* cultivating a *vision of an emptiness* that is not established as anything?

Madhyamika: It is necessary to behold emptiness, *because it is taught in the* 'Perfection of Wisdom' *scriptures* (Prajnaparamita Sutras) *that without the path* of the wisdom that understands emptiness, *there will be no* resultant *Awakening.*[45]

Vaibashika: (41) *However, since the Mahayana* (teachings) *are not* the word of Buddha, they *are not established* as a credible scriptural authority for us.

Madhyamika: Then *how are your scriptures established* as credible?

Vaibashika: They are credible *because they are established* as the word of Buddha for both of us.

Madhyamika: Then *at first,* prior to your acceptance of your tenets, your scriptures cannot have been the word of Buddha, because at that time they were *not established* as the word of Buddha *for you.*

Vaibashika: Nevertheless, they are still credible because we learn about them from a pure unbroken lineage.

Madhyamika: (42) *Yet this reason for which you believe in your* scriptures *is equally* (applicable) *in the Mahayana,* because we too have an unbroken lineage of teachers. Furthermore, *if* you accept something as *true* simply *because two people accept it,* then you should *also accept the Vedas and other* non-Buddhist scriptures *as true,* credible scriptures.

Vaibashika: (43) *The Mahayana* scriptures are not credible *because* they are *disputed.*

Madhyamika: *However, since all your scriptures are disputed by the non-Buddhist and some of them by other Buddhist* schools, you *should reject* your own scriptures, too. (44) *You accept*[46] *any teaching which can be classified into the three scriptural categories* (Tripitaka) as the word of the Buddha, according to whether it discusses the higher training of moral discipline, concentration or wisdom. *If this is so,* since these three trainings are taught in *most Mahayana scriptures* such as the 'Samdhinirmochana Sutra', they are therefore *similar to your* scriptures. *Why* then *do you not accept them* as the word of the Buddha? (45) *If, because of your not recognizing one* scripture such as a 'Prajnaparamita Sutra' as having the complete characteristics of Buddha's speech, you say that *all* Mahayana texts *are corrupt, then,* for the same reason, *because one text* such as the 'Samdhinirmochana Sutra' *is similar* to your texts in having all the characteristics of Buddha's speech, *why not* say that *all* Mahayana texts were *spoken by the Conqueror?*

Vaibashika: If Mahayana texts such as the 'Prajnaparamita Sutras' were the word of Buddha, surely the Great Kashyapa and the other Arhats would have understood them. Since they did not, they cannot be the word of the Buddha.

Madhyamika: Since they are extremely profound, (46) *even the Great Kashyapa and the other* Arhats *could not fathom the depths of* what was expressed in *the teachings* of the Mahayana scriptures. Therefore, just *because you do not understand them, who would regard this* as a reason *for not accepting them* as the word of the Buddha? You say that (47) *the monk* Arhat *is the root* for establishing the presence *of the* Buddha's *teaching, but it would be hard* for those whose minds still apprehend (true existence) and have not understood emptiness *to be monk Arhats*, because they could not have fully abandoned their disturbing conceptions. Therefore, since they would not have abandoned suffering, *it would be hard* for them *to have* attained *the state beyond sorrow* (Nirvana).

Vaibashika: Although they do not understand such an *emptiness*, (48) *they are freed* from suffering *because they have abandoned their disturbing conceptions* by means of meditating upon such things as impermanence and personal identitylessness.

Madhyamika: However, because of having abandoned their misconceptions, *do they become* devoid of suffering *as soon as they* attain the state of an Arhat with residue?[47] *Although those* Arhats *have no disturbing conceptions*, it was clearly taught that *through the latent force of their* previous *actions*, Arhats such as Maudgalyayana *experienced* suffering.

Vaibashika: Although they (49) *temporarily* are not freed from suffering, as soon as they abandon their disturbing conceptions, they will be freed when they leave their bodies because *they definitely do not have any craving* for the aggregates of body and mind, which is *a principal condition* for conditioned existence.

Madhyamika: Yet *while they* still *have* a form of craving that is a *completely undisturbing* state of *confusion*,[48] *why would* they *not* take rebirth with aggregates contaminated by actions and disturbing conceptions? (50) They would, *because the causal condition* of having *feelings* associated with the apprehension of true existence definitely *produces craving*, and these (so-called) Arhats do have such feelings. Since a mind *that lacks the understanding of emptiness is a mind that still apprehends* (true existence), *it will* still conceive of *some objects* (as truly existent). (51) *Although* its manifest (disturbing conceptions) may temporarily *cease, they* *will* nevertheless *arise again in the same way that, during the equipoise of non-discernment,*[49] (disturbing conceptions) temporarily cease only to arise again later (when the period of equipoise is over). *Therefore,* those who wish to put an end to all suffering *should meditate on emptiness.*

When one understands emptiness, compassion should arise (52) *for those* who experience *suffering* as a result of *being confused* about emptiness. Then, *while remaining in cyclic existence, to accomplish* inconceivable benefit for others by means of *liberating them from the* two *extremes of desiring* the happiness of cyclic existence *and fearing* suffering, *is the fruit of* meditating on *emptiness.*

(53) *The remedy for the darkness of the obscurations of disturbing conceptions, as well as the obscuration to the knowable, is* meditation on *emptiness. Therefore, why do those who wish to quickly* obtain *omniscience not meditate on emptiness?* (54) *Since* understanding emptiness has such advantages and not understanding it has such disadvantages, *it is quite invalid to aim criticism in the direction of emptiness.* Therefore *without any doubts* as to whether it is the path of the Buddha or not, *one should* meditate on emptiness.

Objection: I do not want to meditate upon emptiness, because it frightens me.

Reply: (55) *It would* be correct *to be afraid of that which* actually *produces suffering,* the apprehension of *true existence,* but *why be afraid of* meditating on *emptiness if it pacifies* all *suffering?*

II. INTRODUCING THE OBJECT OF MEDITATION : IDENTITYLESSNESS

A. THE IDENTITYLESSNESS OF THE PERSON

1. A General Refutation of Personal Identity

(56) *If a* (truly existent) *self existed,* it would be justifiable *to be afraid of any object at all, but since such a self does not exist, who is*

there to become afraid? (57) *Teeth, hair and nails are not the self, the self is not bones nor blood; it is neither mucus nor is it phlegm; nor is it lymph nor pus.* (58) *The self is not fat nor sweat; the lungs and liver also are not the self; neither are any of the other inner organs; nor is the self excrement or urine.* (59) *Flesh and skin are not the self; warmth and energy-winds are not the self; neither are bodily cavities the self; and at no time are the six types of consciousness the self.* The reason for this is because all six psychophysical categories are impermanent, multiple and not autonomous.

2. A Refutation of the Self Postulated by the Samkhya School

(The Samkhya school is a non-Buddhist tradition of philosophy founded in ancient India by the Rishi Kapila. The followers of this system believe that all phenomena—except the permanent and unchanging self—are created from an all-pervading primal substance (*prakrti*). When the self comes into contact with this primal substance, a series of manifestations such as the intellect, the sense faculties and the objects of the senses issue forth from it, and are then experienced by the self. The primal substance is a permanent, partless and universal material which creates and is the nature of phenomena in the experienced world. The self is the unchanging consciousness principle that becomes bound to the world through its false identification with the manifestations of the primal substance.)[50]

Madhyamika: (60) *If the consciousness that apprehends sound were a permanent* (self), *there would be a* conscious *apprehension of sound at all times* even when sound was absent. Since the consciousness of sound is dependent upon sound, *if there were no* sound as an *object of consciousness, for what* reason and through the cognition of what object *could it be called a consciousness that* apprehends sound? (61) *If there can be a consciousness that* apprehends sound, *even though there is no consciousness* of sound, *it would* (absurdly) *follow that even a piece of wood could become a consciousness* of sound. *Therefore, without an object of consciousness* *remaining close by, we can definitely say that there is no consciousness* that apprehends it.

Samkhya: When there is no sound, it does not mean that there is no apprehender of it because, at a later time when no sounds are present, (62) *the* previous consciousness of *sound becomes consciousness of visual forms* and so forth. These two consciousnesses are one thing.

Madhyamika: *In* this case, *at the time of that* consciousness of visual-form *why is no* sound *heard?*

Samkhya: It is not heard *because no sound exists in the proximity.*

Madhyamika: *Therefore a conscious apprehension of it could not possibly exist.* (63) *How can something whose nature it is to apprehend sound ever apprehend visual forms?* It could not, because their aspects are mutually exclusive.

Samkhya: Their aspects are mutually exclusive, but in relation to two objects occurring at different times, it is not contradictory to say that it is one (consciousness) apprehending them. This is *like one person* who, in relation to his father and his son respectively, is posited *as a son and a father.*

Madhyamika: However, in your tradition *it is not really true to consider* a father and a son as one person because, (64) *in this case,* the truly existent matter (primal substance) which you accept as a non-appearing, equally balanced state of *purity* (sattva), *activity* (rajah) *and darkness* (tamah) *could be neither a father nor a son* (because it has true, independent existence).[51]

The apprehension of a visual-form does not exist as *an apprehension of sound* because if it existed *with that nature* it would surely be apparent, whereas it *is never seen* as such (by a valid cognition).

Samkhya: For example, (65) *just as one actor* has many different roles, *the* previous apprehension of sound *is* later *seen in another way,* i.e. as an apprehension of visual-form.

Madhyamika: Then *the* consciousness *can no longer be permanent,* because it keeps on changing into something else.

Samkhya: Although (the consciousness) appears in *other ways, its* nature remains the same as before and is permanent.

Madhyamika: *Such a oneness* (of nature) *is a* type of *oneness* that you have *never* asserted *before.*

Samkhya: Consciousness appears (66) *in other ways,* and although the (different modes) are *not true,* (their nature) is one and true.

Madhyamika: *Please tell us,* what is this *nature* that is one and true?

Samkhya: It is the nature of *merely being conscious* that is one and true.

Madhyamika: *In that case, it would follow that* the minds of *all* different *individuals are* one because they too are similar in merely being conscious. Furthermore, (67) *the self that has intentions and the* primal substance *that has no intentions would also become one,* because *they are similar in merely being existent,* knowable entities. *When particular* consciousnesses—the apprehensions of sounds, visual forms and so forth—*are mistaken* and untrue, *how can they have* one true general aspect, namely *a similar basis* of merely being consciousness? They cannot, because it is illogical for the general aspect of something to be true when all the particular aspects are false.

3. A Refutation of the Self Postulated by the Naiyayika School

(The Naiyayika accept a permanent, partless, material phenomenon within the being of an individual as the self. This self is claimed to be able to experience objects because it is endowed with a separate mind.)[52]

Madhyamika: (68) Furthermore, *a non-mental phenomenon cannot be the self* that experiences objects *because it lacks* the nature of *mind, just like a jug.*

Naiyayika: *Although* it is itself not of the nature of the mind, it does experience objects because of *being endowed with a* separate *mind.*

Madhyamika: This is illogical, for *when* a self, by nature not conscious of objects, comes to be *conscious* of them through being endowed with a mind, it would absurdly follow that (in becoming a conscious self) the *nonconscious* self *would perish, and* hence *no longer be permanent* (as you assert). (69) *Even if the self were unchanging* then *how, through* being endowed with *a mind, could a* self, which is not conscious of objects, come to be conscious of them? This would not be possible. *Thus*, if you accept as the self something that *is not conscious* of objects because it is matter, and *separated from the function* of producing effects because it is permanent, then *space would also be a self.*

4. Rejection of Arguments Concerning Identitylessness

Question: (70) *If the self were not* permanent, *the relation between the action and its effect*, i.e. the doer of the action coming to experience the results of the actions committed, *would not be maintained.* This is so because *the doer would perish as soon as the action was committed*, and would not exist when the time came to experience the effects (of his action). Therefore *whose action would that be* (to experience)?

Answer: (71) *The basis for the* causal *action*—the aggregates of this life—*and* the basis for *the* ripening *effect*—the aggregates of the future life—*are distinct* states of being. And since in both *these* states *it is established both for you*, because you accept a permanent self, and for us, because we accept identitylessness, *that the self neither commits* the action nor experiences the effect, *is it not meaningless to argue on this point?*

Objection: What about actions whose fruits will be experienced in this life? They do not have different bases (aggregates) upon which the causal action is committed and the result is experienced.

Answer: Nevertheless, in the (same) moment (72) *it is impossible to see* the aggregates of someone committing a *causal* action *being subject* to the experience of *its result*; just as a father and his son cannot be born at the same time.

Objection: However, it says in one scripture:

"How will someone else experience the results of the actions one commits? O monks, the actions you commit and accumulate will not ripen on such things as the external earth element, but upon (your future) aggregates grasped (by consciousness)."

Thus, does not your assertion contradict this statement that the doer of the action must experience its results himself?

Answer: This statement is to be interpreted as follows: while actually *considering the same continuity* (of the individual, the Buddha) *taught that the doer* of the action *is the experiencer* of the result in order to prevent people denying the law of karmic cause and effect. Actually this is not so, because a permanent self is non-existent.

Question: Why is there no permanent self?

Answer: (73) *Neither the mind of the past nor the mind of the future are the self because they are non-existent*; one has ceased and the other has not yet been produced.

Question: *Yet isn't the mind* of the present (moment), which has been *produced* but has not yet ceased, *the self?*

Answer: (If this were the case), then in the next moment, *when it had perished, it would no* longer *be the* self. With this reasoning, all five aggregates are rejected as being the self. (74) *For example, when the trunk of a plantain tree is split into parts there is no* essence found *at all. Likewise, when analytically searched for* with reasoning, a truly existent *self cannot be* found (among the aggregates).

Question: (75) *If there were no sentient beings, towards whom could compassion be developed?*

Answer: Although sentient beings do not truly exist, deceptively one should develop compassion *for those imputed* (as sentient beings) *by the confused mind which has promised* to practice the (Boddhisattva) way of life *in order to* lead them to *the goal* of liberation.

Question: (76) Yet *if sentient beings do not exist, who* will obtain the *results* of developing compassion?

Answer: Although ultimately *it is true* (that there are no truly existent sentient beings, compassion or results), deceptively, *from* the point of view of *a mind confused* about phenomena, *we accept* the existence of merely apparent results arising from merely apparent compassion developed towards merely apparent sentient beings.

Objection: Since compassion is both a subjective state to which things appear in a false way and a mind confused about phenomena, surely it is equally fit to be rejected as is confusion about the self.

Answer: *In order to completely pacify suffering* one need not and cannot reject compassion. Therefore *one should not reject* this merely apparent *confusion about the results.* However, (77) *the confusion about the self* should be rejected because it *increases* such things as *self-importance, which are causes for* suffering.

Objection: *Yet there are no* means to *reject* this confusion.

Answer: There are, because *the supreme remedy* for it *is meditation upon identitylessness.*

B. THE IDENTITYLESSNESS OF PHENOMENA

1. Close Placement of Mindfulness on the Body

(78) *The body is neither feet nor calves; thighs and the waist are not the body; the abdomen and back are not the body; and neither are the chest and shoulders the body.* (79) *The ribs and the hands are not the body; armpits and the nape of the neck are not the body; all inner organs are not the body; neither the head or the neck are the body.* Therefore, what truly existent body is there among these parts?

(80) *If the body abided in all* its limbs equally *in all directions, indeed I* could say that *all the parts* of the body *abide in the parts*

of its limbs, *but where could the* partless, truly existent *body itself abide?* (It would have to exist independent of its parts and unrelated to them.) (81) *And if the entire, truly existent body abided* separately *in each* of the individual *parts, such as the hands, then there would have to be as many bodies as there were parts.* (82) *If there is no* truly existent *body outside or within, how could the hands and so forth have such a body at all? Also, since it is not* something *different from the hands and other parts, how could a* separate *body,* unrelated to its parts, *exist?*

Therefore (83) *the body is not* truly existent, but *through being confused about its hands and other parts, a mind* that mistakes them for a (truly existent) *body arises.* However, the body does not truly exist in the way it is apprehended by that mind. It is like *the mind* apprehending *a pile of stones as a man because of their being set up in a form* similar to a man's. (84) *In the same way* that a pile of stones will *appear to be a man for as long as the causal conditions* to mistake them for a man are assembled, *so will the hands and so forth appear as a* (truly existent) *body for as long as* the causal conditions to mistake them for a body *are present.*

(85) *Just as* the body as a whole is not truly existent, *how can the hands* be truly existent? *They are* only *a composite of fingers.* The fingers, too, are not truly existent *because they are a collection of joints, and the joints,* in turn, *by being divided into their parts,* are also found to be not truly existent. (86) Likewise then *these parts are divided into atomic particles and the atomic particles into their directional parts,* they are revealed as multiples and thus cannot be truly existent units. *Even* when the *directional parts are divided up,* they *are* found to be *devoid of* truly existent *parts. Hence they are* found to be as empty *as space,* and *so even atomic* particles can have no true existence. Thus, although the body appears to be truly existent, in fact it is not. (87) *Therefore who, having analyzed it, would be attached to this dream-like form?* And *when in this way the body is not* truly existent, *how can* the distinction be made into (truly existent) *male and female* bodies?

2. Close Placement of Mindfulness on Feelings

Madhyamika: (88) *If* feelings of *pain truly existed*, then since they would never end, *why would they not affect* feelings of *great joy* and happiness, making it impossible for them ever to arise? Conversely, *if happiness* had true existence, *why do those suffering greatly from grief* and sickness *not find* any *joy in delicious* foods and the like? They should, if happiness had true independent existence, but they clearly do not.

Answer: Indeed pain really exists, but (89) *when a strong* feeling of pleasure *occurs, the pain is not experienced because it is overridden* by the pleasure.

Madhyamika: Yet, simply because it lacks the defining characteristic of a feeling, namely experience, *how can something which is not of the nature of an experience be a feeling?*

Answer: It is feeling because (90) *there is an experience of a very subtle pain. Surely only the gross* aspect *of suffering is dispelled* by the strong pleasure. The nature of this subtle pain is a slight, *weak feeling of happiness distinct from the* gross sensation of pleasure.

Madhyamika: However, *this subtle* experience cannot possibly be a form of pain because you now say it is a form of happiness. (No experience can be simultaneously pleasurable and painful.) (91) *If pain is not occurring* in someone's mind *because its opposite is occurring*, then *to consider* what has not occurred *to be a feeling is surely what could only be called* a mistaken *conception*.

(92) *Therefore*, as *a remedy for such* mistaken conceptions, *one should cultivate the* wisdom which *analyzes* the non-true existence of all phenomena. *The state* of absorption that arises from the field of what is *examined* by this mind *is the nourishment* that sustains *the yogi's understanding of the way things* exist.

(There now follows a refutation of the non-true existence of contact, the cause of feeling. In the first three stanzas (93-95), the argument is directed against those who assert partless atomic particles.)

Madhyamika: (93) *If there were space between the sense faculties such as the eyes and the objects* such as visual forms, *how could the two ever meet?* They would be like a mountain in the east and a mountain in the west. *If there were no space* at all, then since they would become *one unit, what could meet what?* There would be no meet-er and nothing to be met with. Furthermore, (94) the (partless) *atomic particles* of the sense *faculty and the* (partless) *atomic particles* of the object *cannot meet* on all sides, because they cannot enter into one another (i.e., they cannot merge into one another). This is so because atomic particles have *no space* inside *and* are completely *equal* in size. Were they to meet, they would have to do so in this way, because *without one* (partless) atomic particle *entering* into another, there could be no mixing of the two, *and without* this *mixing there could not* possibly *be any meeting* on all sides. (95) *And how would it be logical for* those who accept the existence of a *partless* atomic particle *to say that it is met* on one particular side by another (partless) atom? If that were the case, the partless atomic particle would have one part which is met with, and another part which is not met at all. (Hence it would no longer be partless.) *However, if you ever see* an atomic particle *that has no parts but can* still be *met with, please* show it to us!

It also follows that (96) *it is illogical to meet consciousness* because *it is not physical.* (Something physical cannot possibly meet something non-physical).

Objection: Although there is no physical meeting, there does exist a mere aggregation (of the sense faculty, the object and consciousness) to produce the effect (of a cognition).

Answer: This is invalid *because, just as we analyzed before, an aggregation is not* found to be a truly existent *thing.*[53]

(97) *If in this way contact,* the cause for feeling, *is not* (truly) *existent, from what do* (truly existent) *feelings,* the effect, *arise?* Thus *what is the purpose of tiring oneself out* for the sake of obtaining pleasurable feelings? *And* likewise, *whose* mind *could be caused any harm by what* painful feelings? Both the pleasure which is obtained and the pain which harms have no true existence.

(98) *When there is no* (truly existent) *identity of the person that feels and no* (truly existent) *feelings either, having seen this situation, why do I not turn away the craving* to obtain pleasure and to be separated from pain?

Since the sense objects that (99) *I see and touch* appear to me but have no true existence, *their nature is like a dream and an illusion.* Therefore, the subjective feelings of them can also have no true existence. *Feelings are not seen* (or experienced) *by the mind* which arises simultaneously with them because, since *they are produced simultaneously with it,* they would be (causally) unrelated to it. (100) Likewise, *previous* feelings *and later* feelings *can be remembered* and wished for, *but they cannot actually be experienced* by the mind because they have either ceased or are yet to be produced. Because there would be no experiencer and nothing experienced, *they cannot experience themselves,* and if (one's own mind) of the past, present and future (cannot experience them), *nothing else can experience them either.* (101) *Therefore no* (truly existent) *experiencer of feelings exists and thus no truly existent feelings exist either. So how can this identityless collection* of aggregates be benefitted by pleasurable feelings and *harmed* by painful ones? It cannot, because beneficial and harmful feelings do not truly exist.

3. Close Placement of Mindfulness on the Mind

(102) *A* (truly existent) *mental consciousness does not abide in the sense faculties* such as the eyes, *it does not* abide *in* the objects *such as visual forms, and* it does *not* abide *in between* the two. *Neither does a* (truly existent) *mind exist either inside or outside* the body, *and it is not to be found elsewhere.* (103) *This* (mind) *is neither the body nor* truly *other* than it; *it is not mixed* with it *nor entirely separate* from it; the mind *is not in the slightest bit* truly existent. *Therefore* all *sentient beings* have from the very beginning been *in the natural Nirvana* (i.e. their minds have always been devoid of true existence).

Question: Although the mental consciousness may exist in that way, don't the five sense consciousnesses truly apprehend their five objects?

Answer: Well, let us first consider whether they exist prior to, simultaneously with or after their objects. (104) *If* we said that *the* five *sense consciousnesses existed before the* five *objects of which they are conscious, then, having referred to what objects could those consciousnesses arise?* At that time there could be no objects because they would still have to be produced. Even *if the consciousness and what it is conscious of* arose *simultaneously*, still, *having referred to what object could the consciousness arise?* In this case, when the consciousness is yet to be produced so is its object, and once it has been produced there would be no need for it to be produced by an object.

(105) *And if* the consciousness came into existence *after the object of which it is conscious, then from what* object *could it arise?* Since the object would have ceased by the time the consciousness arose, the consciousness would have no object.

4. Close Placement of Mindfulness on Phenomena

In this way, by means of the above reasoning, *one will come to understand that all phenomena do not* truly *arise.*

5. Rejection of Arguments

Objection: (106) *If, in this way,* all phenomena do not arise; since *there would be no deceptive truths* which arise and perish, *how could two truths be* presented *in the* Madhyamika tradition? *Furthermore, if* all phenomena existed in this way and *deceptive* truths were posited merely through being imputed as arising and perishing entities *by* beings who have a deceived mind, *how could sentient beings pass from sorrow* into Nirvana? They could not, because even though some beings have entered (the unchanging state of) Nirvana, it could become a (changing,) deceptive truth through others simply imputing it to be an arising and perishing entity.

Reply: In reality it is unchanging, but through not understanding this it can be misconceived of as arising and perishing. Just because it is posited as a deceptive truth with regard to that particular (false) conception, this does not imply that it ceases to exist (as an unchanging state). That (false conception) cannot cause Nirvana to no longer exist, because another person cannot make something else a deceptive truth out of his own deception. (107) *This* deception *is a distorted conception* in the mind *of someone* who has not passed into the state beyond sorrow; *it is not the deceptive mind of one* who has passed beyond sorrow. *Later*, when the state of Nirvana is attained, *if that* deceptive conception *were ascertained* to exist, (Nirvana) *would exist* (as) a (changing,) *deceptive truth*; but *since this* (deceptive conception) *does not* exist (in the mind of one who has attained Nirvana), *Nirvana does not exist* (as a changing,) *deceptive truth.*

Objection: (108) *Since the examining mind and the examined object are mutually dependent* upon one another, if the object is not established, the mind, too, would be non-existent. Therefore your analysis (of non-true existence) would be invalid.

Reply: Indeed, because the object does not truly exist, the mind does not truly exist, but this does not mean that the analysis is invalid, because *all analytic minds* are spoken of as conventional consciousnesses and *are said to be dependent upon* reasoning *which is accepted* in the world. (109) *If it were necessary to analyze the analytic mind with* another truly existent *analytic mind, then that analytic mind, too, would have to be analyzed* by yet another analytic mind. *Therefore*, since this process would *never* reach *an end*, the basic object of analysis would never be ascertained. (110) *When the object of analysis has been analyzed* and established to be empty, *the analytic mind is* found *not to have a* (truly existent) *object as its basis* (or reference). Thus *because* (it is understood that) *there is no* truly existent *object*, even without analysis (it is understood that) a truly existent analytic mind *cannot arise* from it. *This* state of peace in which no truly existent objects nor consciousnesses arise *is called Nirvana*, the state beyond sorrow.

III. NEGATING THE CONCEPTION TO BE ELIMINATED: THE APPREHENSION OF TRUE EXISTENCE

A. REFUTING THE TRUE EXISTENCE OF SUBJECT AND OBJECT

(111) *According to* the Realists,[54] *both* the object and the consciousness of it *have true existence.* However, *they are in a very difficult position* because there is no proof for their assertion, whereas it can be refuted.

Realist: The true existence of *the object is established from the* truly existent *sense faculties* of consciousness.

Madhyamika: *What can be* established as truly existent *in dependence upon* a truly *existent consciousness?*

Realist: (112) *On the other hand,* we can also say that *consciousness is established* (as truly existent) *from the objects it is conscious of.*

Madhyamika: *What can depend upon a* (truly) *existent object of consciousness? If they mutually* (truly) *existed through the force of* one another, then when one is not established (as truly existent), the other will also not be (so) established. And in that case, *they would both be non-*(truly) *existent.* For example, (113) *if* someone has *no son,* he *cannot be* established *as a father,* and also if there is no one established as the father, *where can the child come from?* In this way, since *without a child there is no father* and without a father no child, in both cases there can be neither. *Likewise* the object and the consciousness *cannot exist* independently of one another.

Realist: On the contrary, through dependence we can establish things as truly existent. For example, (114) *since a sprout is produced from a seed we can understand* the (true) existence of *the seed from the* sprout even though the sprout depends upon it. Likewise, *why can we not understand that there is a* (truly) *existent* object of consciousness *from the consciousness which is produced from it?*

Madhyamika: This is not the same thing. (115) *The existence of the seed can be understood b; seeing the sprout (that resulted from it) with a consciousness that is other* (than the sprout).

Yet what mind *can understand a truly existent consciousness that understands* (and has arisen from) a truly existent *object of consciousness?* It is impossible to cognize a truly existent consciousness (since such a thing does not exist).

B. ESTABLISHING EMPTINESS OF TRUE EXISTENCE FROM THE VIEWPOINT OF THE CAUSE

1. Refuting Production from No Cause

The (non-Buddhist) Charvakas[55] assert that all things are produced from no cause, because in one of their scriptures it states,

> "All things such as the rising of the sun, the flowing of water downhill, the roundness of peas, the sharpness of thorns and the tail feathers of the peacock were not made by anyone, they arise from their own nature."

Madhyamika: This assertion is unacceptable because (16) *sometimes* the production of an effect from the collection *of all its causes can be seen even by the true perceptions of worldly people.* (Furthermore) it is understood through inference that *the variety* among effects, *such as the different stems of lotus flowers, is produced because of* their having *a variety of causes.*

Charvaka: (117) *Yet by what has this variety of causes been made?*

Madhyamika: *By a variety of previous causes.*

Charvaka: For *what reason is a* distinct *cause able to produce a* distinct *effect?*

Madhyamika: *This comes from the force of its previous cause.*

2. Refuting Production from a Permanent Cause

The (non-Buddhist) Naiyayikas and Vaisheshikas believe the cause of everything to be the god Ishvara. He has five qualities, namely: divinity, purity and being worthy of veneration, permanence, oneness and being the creator of everything.

Madhyamika: (118) *If you* accept *Ishvara* to *be the cause of all beings*, then, *one moment please: who* exactly is Ishvara?

Naiyayika: *He is the* great *elements* of earth, water, fire, air and space.

Madhyamika: *Indeed* these elements are the cause of whatever is formed from them, *but why tire yourselves out over the mere name* 'Ishvara' that you have to them? This is not worth arguing about. In any case, with this assertion you contradict your own definition of Ishvara, because (119) *since earth and the other* great elements *are multiple, impermanent, without* conscious *movement, not divine, something trodden upon and unclean, they cannot be Ishvara.* (120) *Space,* too, *is not Ishvara because it is unmoving,* and *the self* is not him either *because it has already been refuted above.* Furthermore, *if we cannot conceive of the creator* Ishvara, *what is the point of trying to describe this inconceivable entity?* Moreover, exactly (121) *what* effects *is Ishvara asserted to produce?*

Naiyayika: He creates *the self*, the atomic particles of the *earth* element *and so forth, as well as* the later continuity of *himself.*

Madhyamika: *Yet don't* you accept *the nature* of these things *to be permanent?* If you do, it is contradictory to say that they are produced. *Consciousness* (is not produced by Ishvara); its particular states *arise from the* various *objects of consciousness*, and its mere cognitive nature arises from (122) *a beginningless series* of previous cognitions. *Pleasure and pain*, too, *are produced from* wholesome and unwholesome *actions*, respectively. *Therefore* please tell me *what* effects *are produced* by Ishvara. *If the cause,* Ishvara, the permanent producer of effects, *has no beginning, how can the effects of* pleasure and so forth *have a beginning?* Similarly, since Ishvara also has no end, (123) *why* would pleasure and pain *not always exist?* According to you, they should exist in this way, but in reality they are clearly occasional phenomena.

Naiyayika: It is not necessary that Ishvara always produces effects, because although he is permanent, he depends upon other, occasional conditions in order to produce them.

Madhyamika: Yet it would follow that Ishvara *cannot depend upon anything else* because *there are no* phenomena *other* than those *that have been created by* him. *Therefore upon what does* his production of effects *depend?* (124) *If he depended upon a group* of other conditions, it would follow that *those* conditions *themselves would become the cause instead of Ishvara.* This is so because, *once* the causes and conditions were *assembled,* Ishvara would have *no power not to produce* the effects, *and without these* (other causes and conditions) he would have *no power to produce* effects. (125) *If* effects were produced *without the desire of Ishvara, it would follow that they were under the power of something other* than him. *Even if* effects were created *according to his desires, their production would be dependent* upon his desires. And if his *creation were dependent, what would become of* (your permanent, independent) *Ishvara?* He would be under the power of impermanent desires.

(In addition,) (126) the Vaisheshikas *assert* that both the animate and inanimate worlds are produced by *permanent atomic particles. This* assertion cannot be accepted because *we have already refuted* permanent atomic particles *above.*[56]

The Samkhyas believe that all knowable entities can be classified under the conscious self and the material primal substance (together with its manifestations). Among these two, the self is neither a cause nor an effect, whereas the permanent, partless, material, invisible and all-creating *primal substance is asserted to be the cause of the world.* (127) *They speak of a balanced state of the three qualities* (triguna) of equanimity, pleasure and pain, *called* (in their system) *'purity'* (sattva), *'activity'* (rajah), *'darkness'* (tamah), *as being the primal substance. And* they speak of *imbalanced states* of these three qualities, i.e. all states that manifest from the initial imbalance of the primal substance, *as being the world.*

Madhyamika: (128) *This* primal substance you accept *cannot be existent, because it is impossible for something that is* truly *partless to truly exist with a threefold* nature. *Likewise, the qualities cannot* truly *exist* as three *because each of them has three* aspects. This latter reason is established because you accept that every truly existent (manifest) phenomenon has the nature of the three qualities. Furthermore (129) *if the three qualities—the* cause—*do not* (truly) *exist, the existence of* the phenomena, *such as sound,* that are manifested from them as effects *becomes extremely far-fetched.*

It is not possible for clothing and the like (i.e. tactile sensations, visual forms, sounds, etc.) *to have* the same nature of *pleasure and so forth,* because they have *no conscious* quality. (They are manifestations of the primal substance which is matter.)

Samkhya: (130) *Things* such as clothing have (the nature of) pleasure and so forth because they truly *are of the nature of their cause,* namely (the qualities of) pleasure, pain and equanimity (from which they became manifest).

Madhyamika: However, *things* such as clothing are similar to the body (in being composed of parts), and *have we not already refuted* (the true existence) *of the body with our analysis?*[57] Furthermore, in *your* tradition the *cause* for clothing and so forth *is* asserted to be the three qualities of *pleasure and so forth.* (How can this be?) *Woollen cloth does not arise from pleasure.* (On the contrary,) even conventionally, it is seen that (131) *pleasure arises from woollen cloth.* Moreover, upon analysis *the* woollen cloth—the cause—(is found to) have *no* true *existence* and *therefore pleasure,* its effect, can also have *no* true *existence.*

Pleasure and the other feelings *can never be* (validly) *apprehended as permanent* because they are occasional phenomena. (132) *If pleasure were* always *manifestly present,* then *why is it not* also *experienced* at times when pain is produced?

Samkhya: When pain is produced, pleasure is not experienced because *it becomes* very *subtle.*

Madhyamika: *How can something* permanent *be* sometimes *gross* and sometimes *subtle?* (133) *Since it becomes subtle upon ceasing to be gross, this* alternately *gross and subtle* feeling *must be impermanent. For similar reasons, why do you not accept that all manifest things are impermanent?*

Samkhya: Although the various gross and subtle states of pleasure are impermanent, the nature of pleasure itself is permanent.

Madhyamika: (134) *Since the gross* (and subtle) *forms of pleasure are nothing other than pleasure* itself, and since they are impermanent, *pleasure* itself *clearly must be impermanent* as well.

You accept that something cannot be produced from nothing because it does not exist (in the nothingness), just as oil can never come from sand. (135) *Thus while you do not accept the production of manifest entities* that were previously *non-existent, you do claim that* (manifest entities) *must abide* (at the time of their cause) because, although at that previous time they are in an un-manifest state, later (at the time of the effect) they arise in a manifest form. However, *if the effect abided in the cause, to eat food would be to eat excrement,* and (136) *you should purchase and wear cotton seeds with the money you pay for clothing.*

Samkhya: Although things do exist in this way, *the confused people of the world* do not wear cotton seeds because they *cannot see* clothing in them.

Madhyamika: Yet even Kapila, (the founder of your tradition,) *whom* you accept as a *Knower of Truth,* wore clothing and not cotton seeds. Thus *this* must have been *true* for him as well. Furthermore, because in your tradition (137) a *Knower of* Truth— the effect—*would exist in a worldly person*—the cause—*why do* worldly people *not see* clothing in cotton seeds? It follows that they should.

Samkhya: Indeed a Knower of Truth does exist in its cause, a worldly person, but at the time of being a cause all *the states of* mind of *worldly people are invalid.* Therefore they do not understand (that clothing exists in cotton seeds).

Madhyamika: In that case even the effects (such as food, clothing, Knowers of Truth, etc.) *that they clearly see would be untrue*, because they too would be objects of deceived minds.

Samkhya: (138) *If*, according to you Madhyamikas, even *valid cognitions are not valid* (i.e. deceived), *wouldn't* the emptiness *they understand* also *be false?* It must be. *Therefore meditation upon the ultimate* (truth) *of emptiness* is surely *incorrect.*

Madhyamika: (139) *Without contacting* (i.e. apprehending) *the true existence which* the mind *has imputed, one will not apprehend its non-true existence* (its emptiness).[58] In the same way, without having thought of the son of a barren woman, one cannot consider his death. And because non-true existence is dependent upon true existence, *the non-true existence* that is a negation *of the false existence* also *is clearly false* (i.e. it has no true independent existence). Nevertheless, it is quite valid to meditate on emptiness because it is the remedy that eliminates the apprehension of true existence. For example, (140) *when his child dies in a dream, the* dreamer's *thought of* the child's *non-existence causes the thought of* the child's *existence to cease. Although* the thought of his non-existence *is false*, it still has the ability to abandon the thought of his existence.

3. Summary[59]

(141) *Therefore, when such an analysis is made* with these reasonings, *no* impermanent *thing* (is found to) *exist with no cause, and no individual* cause or condition *or any assembly of conditions* (is found to) *have existed* from the very beginning. (142) *Since* (truly existent phenomena) *do not come* anew *from* (somewhere or something) *else*, in the beginning they are not produced, in the middle they *do not remain*, and in the end *they do not go* elsewhere upon cessation. *How*, then, *are all these things*, which under analysis are not established, although they are *apprehended as true by confused minds, not different from illusions?* They appear to be truly existent, whereas in fact they are not.

4. Establishing that Phenomena Conventionally Arise from Causes

(143) *Whatever* horses and elephants have been *made manifest through* a (magician's) *illusion, and whatever* visual forms and so forth have been *made manifest by causes* and conditions *should be examined as to where they* first *came from*, where they abide in the meantime *and where they go to* in the end. Upon examination they will be found to be similar in not truly coming and going. (144) *An* effect *will only be seen because of* its being closely connected with a cause, *but without* that cause it will *not* be seen. Since it is *a product* of causes and conditions, it is *similar to a reflection* in a mirror, *so how can it have true* (independent) *existence?*

C. ESTABLISHING EMPTINESS OF TRUE EXISTENCE FROM THE POINT OF VIEW OF THE EFFECT

(145) *What would be the need of a cause for a thing that* (truly) *existed?* (If it truly existed), it would already exist. *And what would be the need of a cause for it if it didn't exist at all?* (If it didn't exist), it would not be the effect of anything.

Objection: Although a cause cannot make a non-existent arise *into a non-thing, it can change into a thing.*

Reply: This is illogical; (146) *even by means of a hundred million causes, a non-thing cannot be transformed into anything* else because it is permanent. If it were able to change, it would have to do so either while retaining its non-thingness, or through discarding it. In the former instance, *how could it become a thing* as long *as its condition* remained unseparated from being a non-thing? And in the second instance, *what is there that could* (first) separate itself from the state of a non-thing and then (proceed) *to become a thing?* This is an impossibility. (147) *Furthermore, if* the condition of a non-thing is not discarded, it *will be impossible for a thing to exist at the* same *time.* In which case, *when could a thing ever come to exist?* Also (a further consideration should be made) in the case of a non-thing becoming a thing upon having first discarded the condition of a non-*thing*. *Without actually becoming a thing*, a non-thing *cannot be separated from* the state of a non-*thing*; and (148) *if it has not become separate from this state, it is impossible for the state of an existent thing* to arise. Similarly, a (truly existent) *thing does not become a non-thing* upon cessation, because *it would* absurdly *follow that something with one nature would become twofold* (i.e. both a thing and a non-thing).

(149) *In this way there is no cessation* or production of (truly existent) *things. Therefore all beings never have a* (truly existent) *birth nor a* (truly existent) *cessation.* They are pacified (of true existence) from the very beginning, and by nature in the state beyond sorrow (i.e. in a state devoid of true existence). (150) Although *sentient beings* appear, they *are* not truly existent, just like *a dream. And* since they are found to have no essence *upon analysis*, they *are* also *like* a *plaintain tree. Therefore, in their being* (empty of true existence), *there is no difference between the state beyond sorrow*—Nirvana—*and the state not beyond* sorrow—cyclic existence.

IV. THE RESULTS OF WISDOM

151

What is there to gain and what is there to lose
With things that are empty (of true existence) in this way?
Who is there to pay me respect,
And who is there to abuse me?

152

From what are pleasure and pain derived?
What is there to be happy or unhappy about?
When I search for the ultimate nature,
Who is there to crave, and what is there to crave for?

153

Upon analysis, this world of living beings (is found to have no
    true existence),
Therefore who can die here?

What is there to come and what has been?
Who are friends and who are relatives?

154

O you (who are investigating reality),
Please recognize, as I have done, that all is just like space!
Those who wish to be happy
Are greatly disturbed by causes for conflict
And overjoyed by the causes for pleasure.

155

Not finding happiness, they suffer,
And in order to find it, they exert themselves.
They argue with others, cut and stab one another;
With many wrong deeds, they live in a state of great hardship.

156

Even though they repeatedly come to happy existences
And experience much pleasure there,
Upon dying, they fall for a long time
Into the unbearable sufferings of lower realms.

157

Within conditioned existence, the chasms (of suffering) are many
And the (liberating comprehension of) ultimate truth is absent.
Furthermore (the apprehension of true existence and the under-
    standing of emptiness) mutually contradict one another.
Yet if, while in conditioned existence, I do not
    (realize) this ultimate truth,

158

I shall (continue to experience) a limitless ocean of misery,
Unbearable and beyond analogy.
Likewise, (through not having realized emptiness,) I have little
    strength (for virtue)
And my human life (of leisure and endowment) is indeed very
    short.

159

Also, I strive hard to live long and avoid illness,
I am (concerned with) hunger, rest and sleep;
I am injured by others
And keep meaningless company with the childish.

160

Therefore this life swiftly passes with no meaning,
And it is very hard to find the chance to investigate reality.
In this state, where is there the means to reverse
This beginningless habit of grasping at true existence?

161

Furthermore, devils are exerting themselves
To cast us into vast unfortunate realms,
They show us many mistaken paths
And it is hard to resolve doubts about the perfect way.

162

It will be hard to find the leisure (of a human life) again,
And extremely difficult to find the presence of the Buddhas.
It is hard to forsake this flood of disturbing conceptions.
Alas, sentient beings will continue to suffer!

163

O indeed, it is worth feeling sorrow
For those adrift in the river of pain, who
Although they experience great misery
Are unaware of the sufferings they go through.

164

For example, some (ascetics) wash themselves again and again,
And others repeatedly enter fire,
But although they thereby suffer greatly,
They pride themselves in being content.

165

Similarly, those (who mistake their suffering for joy)
And live as though there were no ageing or death,
Are first of all killed (by the Lord of Death),
And then experience the unbearable misery of falling into lower
  realms.

166

When shall I be able to extinguish
(The pains of) those tormented by the fires of suffering
With the rain of my accumulated happiness
That has sprung from the clouds of my merits?

167

And by having, in the manner of not referring (to true existence),
Respectfully gathered the accumulation of merit,
When, by referring to the other, will I be able to reveal emptiness
To those who are wretched and sad?

CHAPTER X

Dedication

1

Through the virtue of having composed this work,
A Guide to the Bodhisattva's Way of Life,
May all living beings come to engage
In the Bodhisattva's conduct.

2

May all beings everywhere,
Plagued with sufferings of body and mind,
Obtain an ocean of happiness and joy
By virtue of my merits.

3

For as long as they remain in cyclic existence,
May their (mundane) happiness never decline,
And may all of them, uninterruptedly, receive
Waves of joy from Bodhisattvas.

4

May all embodied creatures,
Who throughout the universe
Experience hellish realms,
Come to enjoy the bliss of Sukhavati.

5

May those feeble with cold find warmth,
And may those oppressed with heat be cooled
By the boundless waters that pour forth
From the great clouds of the Bodhisattvas' (merits).

6

May the forest of razor-sharp leaves
Become a beautiful pleasure grove,
And may the trees of knives and swords
Grow into wish-fulfilling trees.

7

May the regions of hell become places of joy
With vast and fragrant lotus pools,
Beautiful, with the exquisite calls
Of wild ducks, geese and swans.

8

May the heaps of burning coals change into heaps of jewels,
May the burning ground become a polished crystal floor,
And may the mountains of the crushing hells
Become celestial palaces of worship, filled with Sugatas.

9

May the rains of lava, blazing stones and weapons
From now on become a rain of flowers,
And may all battling with weapons
From now on be a playful exchange of flowers.

10

By the force of my virtues, may those caught in the fiery
    torrents of acid,
Their flesh eaten away, revealing their lily-white bones,
Obtain the bodies of celestials
And dwell with goddesses in gently flowing rivers.

11

"Why are the henchmen of Yama, the unbearable buzzards and
    vultures afraid?
Through whose noble strength is joy brought upon us and
    darkness dispelled?"

Looking up, they behold in the firmanent the radiant form of
Vajrapani!
Through the force of their joy, may they be free from wrongdo-
ing and find his company.

12

When they see the lava fires of hell extinguished
By a rain of falling flowers mixed with scented water,
Immediately satisfied, they wonder whose work this was;
In this way, may those in hell behold Padmapani.

13

"Friends, don't be afraid but quickly gather here,
What need is there to flee when above us is the youthful
Manjughosha to dispel our fears,
The tender Bodhisattva who protects all living things,
Through whose might all suffering is removed and the force of
joy abounds.

14

"Behold him in an enchanting palace resounding with hymns
sung by a thousand goddesses,
With the tiaras of a hundred gods being offered to his lotus feet,
And a rain of many flowers falling on his head, the eyes of which
are moist with kindness."
Upon seeing Manjughosha in this way, may those in hell cry out
loud with joy.

15

Likewise, having seen, due to the roots of my wholesome deeds,
The cool and sweet-smelling rain falling from joyful clouds
Created by the Bodhisattvas Samantabhadra and Sarva-nirvarana-
vishkambhini,
May all beings in hell be truly happy.

16

May all animals be free from the fear
Of being eaten by one another;
May the hungry ghosts be as happy
As the people of the Northern Continent.

17

May they be satisfied
By a stream of milk pouring from the hand
Of the Noble Lord Avalokiteshvara,
And by bathing in it, may they always be cooled.

18

May the blind see forms,
May the deaf hear sounds,
And just as it was with Mayadevi,
May pregnant women give birth without any pain.

19

May the naked find clothing,
The hungry find food;
May the thirsty find water
And delicious drinks.

20

May the poor find wealth,
Those weak with sorrow find joy;
May the forlorn find new hope,
Constant happiness and prosperity.

21

May all who are sick and ill
Quickly be freed from their illness,
And may every disease in the world
Never occur again.

22

May the frightened cease to be afraid,
And those bound be freed;
May the powerless find power,
And may people think of benefitting one another.

23

May all travellers find happiness
Everywhere they go,
And without any effort, may they accomplish
Whatever they set out to do.

24

May those who sail in ships and boats
Obtain whatever they wish for,
And having safely returned to the shore,
May they joyfully reunite with their relatives.

25

May troubled wanderers who have lost their way
Meet with fellow travellers,
And without any fear of thieves and tigers,
May their going be easy without any fatigue.

26

May those who find themselves in trackless, fearful wilder-
    nesses—
The children, the aged, the unprotected,
Those stupefied and the insane—
Be guarded by beneficent celestials.

27

May beings be free from all states of no leisure
And be endowed with faith, wisdom and kindness;
With food (obtained in a proper manner) and excellent conduct,
May they be mindful throughout their lives.

28

May all beings be without want for wealth
Just like the treasury of space,
And without (it being the source of) dispute or harm,
May they always enjoy it as they wish.

29

May those who have little splendor
Come to be endowed with majesty;
And may those whose bodies are worn with toil
Find magnificent and noble forms.

30

May all lower life-forms in the universe
Take (rebirth) in higher forms;
May the lowly obtain grandeur,
And may the proud be humbled.

31

By the merits I (have accumulated),
May every single being
Abandon all forms of wrongdoing
And perpetually engage in virtue.

32

May they never be parted from the Awakening Mind,
And may they always engage in the Bodhisattva's conduct;
May they be cared for by the Buddhas
And relinquish the actions of devils.

33

May sentient beings have lives
Inconceivably long (when in fortunate realms);
May they always live in contentment,
Unfamiliar with even the word 'death'.

34

May there abound, in all directions,
Gardens of wish-fulfilling trees
Filled with the sweet sound of Dharma
Proclaimed by the Buddhas and their Children.

35

And may the land everywhere be pure,
Smooth and devoid of any rocks,
Level like the palm of the hand,
And of the nature of lapis lazuli.

36

For all the circles of disciples,
May many Bodhisattvas
Dwell in every land,
Adorning them with their excellent (manifestations).

37

May all embodied creatures
Uninterruptedly hear
The sound of Dharma issuing from birds and trees,
Beams of light and even space itself.

38

May they always meet with Buddhas
And their children the Bodhisattvas,
Then may these spiritual masters of the world
Be worshipped with endless clouds of offerings.

39

May celestials bring timely rains
So that harvests may be bountiful.
May kings act in accordance with Dharma,
And the people of the world always prosper.

40

May all medicines be effective
And the repeating of mantras successful;
May dairkin, cannibals and the like
Be endowed with compassionate minds.

41

May no living creature ever suffer,
Commit wrong or ever fall ill.
May no one be afraid or belittled,
Or their minds ever be depressed.

42

In all temples and monasteries
May reading and recitation flourish and remain;
May the Sangha always be in harmony
And may their purposes be accomplished.

43

May monks desiring to practice
Find quiet and solitary places,
And through having abandoned all wandering thoughts,
May they meditate with flexible minds.

44

May nuns be materially sufficient,
Abandon quarrelling (with each other) and be unharmed.
Similarly, may all ordained ones
Never let their morality weaken.

45

Having repented any moral falls
May transgression always be eradicated,
And thereby obtaining a happy state of birth,
May spiritual conduct not decline even there.

46

May the wise be honored
And may they receive alms;
May their minds be completely pure,
And may they be renowned in all directions.

47

May beings not experience the misery of lower realms
And may they never know any hardships;
With a physical form superior to the gods,
May they swiftly attain Buddhahood.

48

May sentient beings, again and again,
Make offerings to all the Buddhas,
And may they constantly be joyful
With the inconceivable bliss of the Buddhas.

49

Just as they intended,
May the Bodhisattvas fulfill the welfare of the world,
And may all sentient beings receive
Whatever the Buddhas have intended for them.

50

Similarly, may the Pratyekabuddhas
And the Shravakas find happiness.

51

And until I reach the level of the Joyous One
Through the kindness of Manjughosha,
May I be mindful throughout my lives,
And always obtain ordination.

52

May I live and be sustained
By simple, common foods,
And in all my lives, may I find
The ideal solitude (for practicing Dharma).

53

Whenever I wish to see something
Or even wish to ask the slightest question,
May I behold without any hindrance
The Lord Manjughosha himself.

54

In order to fulfill the needs
Of beings who reach unto the ends of space,
May my way of life
Be just like that of Manjughosha.

55

For as long as space endures
And for as long as living beings remain,
Until then may I, too, abide
To dispel the misery of the world.

56

May all the pains of living creatures
Ripen (solely) upon myself,
And through the might of the Bodhisattva Sangha,
May all beings experience happiness.

57

May the teachings, which are the sole medicine for suffering
And the origin of every joy,
Be materially supported and honored
And abide for a very long time.

58

I prostrate to Manjughosha
Through whose kindness wholesome minds ensue,
And I prostrate to my spiritual masters,
Through whose kindness I develop.

The Colophon

This concludes *A Guide to the Bodhisattva's Way of Life*, composed by Acharya Shantideva. It was translated (from the Sanskrit into Tibetan), edited and settled upon from a Kashmiri edition by the Indian scholar Sarvajnadeva and the editor-translator monk Pal-tzeg. It was then corrected in accordance with a Magadha edition and commentary, retranslated and settled upon by the Indian scholar Dharmashribhadra and the editor-translator monk Rin-chen Zang-po and Shakya Lo-dro. The once more, at a later time, it was further corrected, retranslated and finalized by the Indian scholar Sumatikirti and the editor-translator monk Lodan Sherab.

It was translated from Tibetan into English by the Buddhist monk Stephen Batchelor in accordance with an oral teaching of Geshe Ngawang Dhargyey, translated by Sharpa Tulku, with the commentary *The Ocean of Good Explanation* by Thog-me Zang-po. The translator acknowledges the work of Dr. Alexander Berzin, who kindly corrected the entire manuscript and made many valuable improvements; and also of Brian Beresford and Glenn Mullin for their helpful suggestions in the editing and presentation of the text.

Notes

1. *Byang-chub-kyi sems*; Skt: *bodhicitta*. A mind infused with the aspiration to attain the state of Buddhahood for the sake of all sentient beings. This is the entrance to and the motivation behind the Bodhisattva's way of life.

2. *Dal-'byor*. This term denotes the perfect condition of human existence, in which one has freedom from eight particularly unfavorable states of being and is endowed with the ten conditions conducive to leading a spiritual life. See Geshe Ngawang Dhargyey, *Tibetan Tradition of Mental Development* (Library of Tibetan Works and Archives, Dharamsala, 1974) p. 42 seq., and sGam-po-pa, trans. H.V. Guenther, *The Jewel Ornament of Liberation* (Shambala, Berkeley, 1971) p. 14 seq.

3. *Gandavyuha Sutra*. Cited in Thog-me Zang-po, *The Ocean of Good Explanation, a Commentary to (Shantideva's) Guide to the Bodhisattva's Way of Life (Byang-chub sems-dpa'i spyod-pa-la 'jug-pa'i 'grel-pa (legs-par bshad-pa'i rgya-mtsho)* (Sarnath, 1974) p. 16 (This text will hereafter be abbreviated as *Thog.*),

'O Noble Son, the Awakening Mind is like the seed of all the Buddhas' qualities. Since it increases the wholesome qualities of all beings it is like a field; since it supports each and every creature, it is like the earth; since it perfectly severs all poverty, it is like the god of wealth; since it affords complete protection to all Bodhisattvas, it is like a father; since it perfectly accomplishes all aims, it is like the king of wish-fulfilling gems; since it completely fulfills all intentions, it is like an auspicious vase...O Noble Son, the

Awakening Mind is endowed with such excellent virtues as these as well as limitless other benefits.'

4. *Subahupariprccha Sutra, Thog.* p. 18,

'If one perseveres for the sake of bringing happiness and benefit to an infinite number of beings, then the infinite roots of virtue from this infinite aim that bears in mind the happiness and benefit of all sentient beings shall increase, expand and reach towards fulfilment every moment, day and night, regardless of whether one is unconscientious or even asleep.'

5. *Prasantaviniscayapratiharya Sutra. Thog.* p. 22,

'O Manjushri, for as many thoughts of anger or contempt that one Bodhisattva bears to another Bodhisattva, for that many aeons shall he remain in hell. Therefore wear armor.'

6. *Thams-cad gtong-bar chabs-gcig la/sems-can rnams-la btang-ba mchog./* Alternatively: 'And along with giving up everything, it is best to give it to all creatures.'

7. *Nyon-mongs*; Skt: *klesha*. This term is variously translated as 'delusion', 'defilement', 'emotion'; but here the term 'disturbing conception' will be employed. The reason for this choice is as follows: According to the *Abhidharmasamuccaya*, a *klesha* is 'a mental factor that, upon occurring in the mind, has the function of producing turmoil in and a lack of control over the psyche.' By adding the term 'conception' (*rtog-pa*), it is being noted that the kleshas are primarily a reflective as opposed to a pre-reflective function of consciousness. 'Conception' should not be understood in the limited sense of intellectual thought, but in a wider sense of any subjectively conditioned mental response, whether emotional, such as in attachment, hatred, or pride, or intellectual, such as in mistaken views, doubts, etc. For further clarification see Geshe Rabten, *The Mind and its Functions*, (Tharpa Choeling, Switzerland, 1978) p. 17 seq. and p. 88 seq.

8. *Saddharmasmrtyupasthana Sutra, Thog.* p. 57,

'If one does not give the slightest thing (one) once intended (to give), one can be born as a hungry ghost; and if one does not give something (one) promised (to give), one can be born in hell.'

9. *Prasantaviniscayapratiharya Sutra, Thog.* p. 59,

'Should one person steal the possessions of and kill every being in the world, and should another obstruct the slightest virtue of a Bodhisattva, such as that of giving a morsel of food to an animal, the transgression of the latter would be incalculably greater than the former. This is so because he would be obstructing the virtue which gives rise to the occurrence of a Buddha.'

10. *Yang dag-par ldan-pa'i lung. Thog.* p. 61 scq.,

'O monks, suppose that this great earth were to become an ocean upon which a single yoke were being tossed about by the wind and thus being moved from here to there. If under that ocean there were a blind turtle, do you think it would be easy for it to insert its head into that yoke when it rises to the surface only once every hundred years?' 'No Lord, it would not,' replied the monks. The Lord then said, 'In a similar fashion, O monks, it is extremely hard to obtain the human state.'

11. *Ratnamegha Sutra, Thog.* p. 71,

'If control is gained over the mind alone, control will be gained over everything.' And, 'Both wholesome and unwholesome actions are accumulated by the mind.'

Also, *Dharmasangiti Sutra, Thog.* p. 71,

'Everything is dependent on the mind.'

12. *Saddharmasmrtyupasthana Sutra, Thog.* p. 72,

'Among enemies, the mind is the greatest enemy. There is no enemy other than it.'

13. *Samadhisamgraha Sutra, Thog.* p. 74,

'O monks, when practiced with a mind distracted to

desire-objects, physical hardships and recitations will bear
no results.'

14. The difference between mindfulness (*dran-pa*; Skt: *smrti*)
and alertness (*shes-bzhin*; Skt: *samprajanya*) is explained as
follows in *Thog*. p. 69 seq.,

'In this context "mindfulness" means to be mindful of all
that one has accepted to relinquish and to cultivate. "Alertness" means to be skilful in applying oneself to this relin-
quishment and cultivation.'

15. *Aksayamatipariprccha Sutra, Thog*. p. 81,

'At times of giving, moral discipline may be condensed;
that is to say, left in a neutral state.'

16. To work in the fields of excellence, benefit and misery
means to direct one's wholesome deeds towards the objects
of refuge (the field of excellence), one's parents, teachers,
etc. (the field of benefit), and those who are suffering (the
field of misery).

17. In some editions of the text 'faith' (*dad-pa*; Skt: *shraddha*) is
found instead of 'joy' (*dga'-ba*; Skt: *priti*).

18. *Phung-po gsum-pa'i-mdo*; Skt: *Triskandha Sutra*. See B.C.
Beresford, ed., *Mahayana Purification* (to be reprinted later
as *Confession of Downfalls*) (Library of Tibetan Works and
Archives, Dharamsala 1992).

19. The biography of Shrisambhava included in the *Gandavyuha
Sutra, Thog*. p. 97,

'One should honor and respect the spiritual friend with a
mind like the earth, which does not become discouraged
although it bears all burdens; like a diamond, indestruc-
tible in its intention; like a mighty fence, which cannot be
breached by any suffering; like a slave, who does not
complain in having to undertake all tasks; like a sweeper,
having relinquished all self-importance; like a vehicle, in
bearing heavy loads; like a pet dog, in not becoming
angry; like a boat, which does not object to coming and

going; and like a wise son, in beholding the face of the spiritual friend.

Noble Son, you should recognize yourself to be a sick man; the spiritual friend to be the doctor; his precepts to be the medicine; and an earnest practice to be the way to treat the sickness.'

20. *bslab-pa kun-las btus-pa*; Skt: *Shikshasamuccaya.* This is a text compiled from various Mahayana sutras by Shantideva himself as a complementary volume to the *Bodhicharyavatara.* See C. Bendall and W.H.D. Rouse, transl. *Shikshasamuccaya— A Compendium of Buddhist Doctrine* (Motilal Banarsidas, Delhi, 1971).

21. *Spyi gtso-bo*; Skt: *prakrti.* According to the non-Buddhist Samkhya school of philosophy, the primal substance is the permanent underlying material cause and the nature of all objective phenomena. For further clarification of this concept see below, p. 75 and 90.

22. *hdag*; Skt: *atman.* This refers to the non-Buddhist concept of an unchanging, partless and autonomous self or soul. For further discussion see Chapter IX, 60-69, pp, 153-7 seq.

23. *Dharmasangiti Sutra, Thog.* p. 126,

'The field of sentient beings is a Buddha field because it is from that Buddha field that the qualities of a Buddha are attained. Hence, in that field, it is incorrect to practice in a mistaken way.'

24. *Subahupariprccha Sutra, Thog.* p. 136,

'Furthermore the Bodhisattva should perfectly train himself in the following way: He should consider that if those who are now lions, tigers, dogs, jackals, vultures, storks, crows, owls, insects, bees and mosquitoes will (in the future) awaken to the unsurpassable Enlightenment; why, while I am a human being, should I degenerate the enthusiasm in attaining Enlightenment even at the cost of my life?'

25. In the root text the term 'appreciation' (*mos-pa*; Skt:

adhimukti) appears, but Thog-me Zang-po, in agreement with the Indian commentary '*Grel-chen* and the Tibetan translator Lama Pang, substitutes 'aspiration' (*'dun-pa*; Skt: *chanda*). See *Thog*. p. 139.

26. The discussion of the support of aspiration is covered in stanzas 31-48, steadfastness in stanzas 49-62, joy in stanzas 63, 66, and rest in stanza 67.

27. *nga-rgyal*; Skt: *mana*. Here this term is equivalent to steadfastness (*brtan pa*), the second support for enthusiasm mentioned in stanza 31. It should not be confused with 'self-importance' also *nga-rgyal*. For this distinction, see Chapter VII, 56-59.

28. *Avatamsaka Sutra, Thog.* p. 144,

'For example, Devaputra, when the sun shines forth it illuminates any suitable place without being turned back by such obstacles as blindness in people or uneven mountain formations. Likewise when a Bodhisattva shines forth for the sake of others he ripens and liberates any suitable disciple and is not turned back by the various obstacles present in sentient beings.'

29. These two lines occur in some editions of the text, but it is not certain whether they are the actual words of Shantideva. See *Thog*. p. 148.

30. *De-bzhin gshegs-pa thams-cad kyi yul-la 'jug-pa, Thog.* p. 157,

'Just as wild animals are never happy in a crowd, there is no satisfaction in involvement with the childish.'

31. *Samadhiraja Sutra, Thog.* p. 176,

'At the time of the decline of the doctrine of the Tathagata Rinpoche Pad-ma'i Da-wa Ngon-par phag-pa'i gyal-po there lived a monk called Supushpachandra. At one time, while dwelling in the Samantabhadra Grove together with seven thousand Bodhisattvas, he perceived with his heightened awareness that if he were to go to the jewelled palace of King Viradatta and reveal the Dharma, many living creatures would obtain higher states of existence and liberation, but if he were not to reveal it they would not obtain these states. In addition, he knew that if he went, the king would kill him, but nevertheless (he decided) to go there. Upon his arrival he spent seven days without partaking of any food; during the night he would circumambulate a reliquary containing the fingernails of the Tathagata, and during the daytime he would go to the palace and reveal the Dharma. After many million living beings had been led to Enlightenment through his teachings, the King then killed him. After a while, though, the King regretted what he had done and subsequently enshrined his bones in a reliquary and worshipped them.'

32. *Gandavyuha Sutra, Thog.* p. 180,

'By recollecting my name three times, may the fear of being embarrassed among people be dispelled.'

33. From stanzas 141 to 154, as a practice of exchanging self for others, the role of 'I' and 'other' is literally reversed. Thus 'I' should be understood as all other sentient beings, and 'he' should be understood as oneself. The meditation on envy is covered in stanzas 141-146, competitiveness in stanzas 147-150, and self-importance in stanzas 151-154.

34. The Madhyamika school was founded by the Buddhist sage Nagarjuna and later clarified by such masters as Aryadeva, Chandrakirti and Shantideva. Their principal tenet is that all phenomena lack true existence (*bden-par grub-pa*; Skt: *satya siddha*), i.e. existence independent of causes, parts or conceptual imputation. Nothing exists from its own side, in an unrelated, objective manner, but solely in dependence upon its causes, its components and conceptualization. The lack of such true existence is called 'emptiness' (*stong-pa nyid*; Skt: *shunyata*) and this is the ultimate truth and nature of each existent phenomenon, towards an understanding of which most of the Madhyamika dialectic is aimed. In the following dialogues, the Madhyamikas, represented by Shantideva, proceed to refute the tenets of certain non-Buddhist and Buddhist schools that reveal this tendency

towards asserting true existence. Thereby the notion of true existence is put into question and its emptiness is demonstrated. See Geshe Lhundup Sopa and Jeffrey Hopkins, *Practice and Theory of Tibetan Buddhism* (Rider, London, 1976), p. 122 seq. (This text will hereafter be abbreviated as *Practice*.) Also see Jeffrey Hopkins, *Meditation on Emptiness* (Wisdom, London, 1983) for extensive information.

35. *Phyi don-du smra-ba*. The Hinayana philosophical schools of the Vaibashikas and Sautrantikas, see *Practice*. p. 70 seq.

36. *sems tsam-pa*. The Mahayana 'Mind-Only' school. See below, p. 142-3 and *Practice*. p. 107 seq.

37. This and many following objections are based upon the assumption that when the Madhyamikas speak of 'no true existence' they are denying existence itself. It must always be emphasized that 'true' existence is a totally false mode of existence bearing no correspondence at all with reality. The Madhyamikas assert that both conventional, deceptive truths as well as ultimate truths exist and are established by valid cognitions. It is only the falsely imagined 'true existence' of phenomena that is non-existent and to be refuted.

38. *mngon-sum*; Skt: *pratyaksha*. Non-mistaken, non-deceptive perception such as occurs in valid sense consciousness, etc. See Geshe Rabten, *The Mind and its Functions* (Tharpa Choeling. Switzerland 1979) p. 11 seq.

39. *Rang-bzhin gyi mya-ngan las 'das-pa*. This does not refer to the state of Nirvana attained by the Arhats and Buddhas, but to the emptiness of true existence. Not understanding the Madhyamika's use of the term, this objection is raised by those who have taken it literally. See Doboom Tulku, *What is Nirvana?* (*Tibet Journal* vol.1, Library of Tibetan Works and Archives, Dharamsala, 1975) p. 87 seq.

40. *Lankavatara Sutra, Thog.* p. 205,

> 'Just as a sword cannot cut its own blade, and just as a finger cannot touch its own tip, likewise the mind cannot see the mind.'

41. *Thog.* p. 206,

'This is the way some Tibetan scholars have explained these lines. However, (the Indian commentator) Sher-jung offers the following explanation: "Blueness does not become blue without depending upon other factors because it depends upon its causes. If it arose from its causes as something not blue and then became blue, it would have to have made itself the nature of blue independently of any other causal conditions. This is impossible because it is contradictory for something to make itself."'

42. In Buddhism, to exist means to be established by a valid cognition. In the Chittamatrin school, forms and so forth are established as existent by valid other-cognitions and the other-cognitions themselves are established by valid self-cognition. If, as the Madhyamikas claim, self-cognition is non-existent, it would follow (for the Chittamatrins) that there would be no consciousness to establish other-cognitions and hence they could not be posited as existent.

43. According to the Chittamatrins, for ordinary beings in cyclic existence the mind and its objects appear to be substantially distinct entities. In reality, however, they are substantially identical. They are both of the nature of mind; one being the subjective knower and the other being an appearing aspect of mind that is known. In this sense, consciousness is 'non-dual.' In addition it is regarded as that which is truly existent and real.

44. For the Madhyamikas, to be truly existent would necessarily imply a mode of existence entirely independent of any other factors.

45. *Prajnaparamita Sutra, Thog.* p. 213,

'He who has a recognition of (truly existent) things has no meditation upon the Perfection of Wisdom... He has no abandonment of disturbing conceptions initiated through previous tendencies.' Also, 'Whoever thinks of becoming a Shravaka Arhat, or whoever wants to become a Pratyekabuddha and likewise a King of Dharma, will not obtain what he wishes without relying upon this forbearance (i.e. the understanding of emptiness).'

46. Stanzas 44 to 51 are arranged according to the order in which they appear in *Thog* and differ somewhat from the order of the root text. There is some dispute as to whether stanzas 44 to 46 were actually composed by Shantideva. See *Thog*. p. 214.

47. *Lhag-bcas kyi dgra bcom-pa*. An Arhat who has not yet left the body that was produced through the force of tainted actions and disturbing conceptions. Once an Arhat dies he/ she becomes an Arhat without residue (*lhag-med kyi dgra bcom-pa*).

48. *Nyon-mongs ma-yin pa'i rmongs-pa*. According to the Hinayanists, the subtle confusion existent in the mind of an Arhat that distinguishes that state of realization from that of a Buddha. See *Practice*. p. 83.

49. *'du-shes med-pa'i snyoms-'jug*. The highest state of formless absorption attainable within cyclic existence.

50. See *Practice*. p. 58 seq.

51. Father and children are established in relation to their children and father respectively, but they do not inherently exist as such. The Madhyamikas accept the example given but point out that when the Samkhyas use it, it is in contradiction to their own assertions. The primal substance is said to be truly (and thus independently) existent. Therefore its existence would not have to be determined as a cause ('father') in relation to its results. It would absurdly become a cause established independently of its results.

52. See *Practice*. p. 56 seq.

53. See above VII: 101, p. 58.

54. *Dngos smra-ba*. Those who maintain that all or some phenomena have true existence. This includes the non-Buddhists, the Vaibashikas, the Sautrantikas and the Chittamatrins. Since the latter are included, this term should not be understood as being the antonym for 'idealist'.

55. See *Practice*. p. 63 seq.

56. See above IX: 93-95.

57. See above IX: 78-87.

58. *btags-pa'i dngos-pa ma-reg par/ de-yi dngos-med 'dzin ma-yin.* Literally: ' Without contacting the thing imputed, there will be no apprehension of its being a non-thing.'

59. This is a summary of sections 1 and 2: the refutations of production from the cause (IX:116-117) and from a permanent cause (IX:118-140).

Glossary

Akashagharbha: (*nam-mkha'i snying-po*) lit: 'the heart of space', the name of a Bodhisattva.

Arhat: (*dgra bcom-pa*) lit: 'one who has overcome the foe', namely one who has overcome the foe of disturbing conceptions and has attained liberation from cyclic existence. In Chapter IX this term refers specifically to the Hinayana Arhat.

Arya: (*'phags-pa*) lit: 'a superior being', one who has attained a direct perception of Ultimate Truth.

Avalokiteshvara: (*'jig-rten dbang-phyug*) lit: 'the lord of the world', the name of the Bodhisattva of Compassion.

Awakening Mind: (*byang-chub kyi sems*, Skt. *bodhicitta*). See note 1.

Bodhisattva: (*byang-chub sems-dpa'*) A being who, having developed the Awakening Mind, devotes their life to the task of achieving Buddhahood for the sake of all sentient beings.

Brahma: (*tshang-pa*) A powerful deity residing in the realm of form.

Brahmin: (*bram-ze*) A person belonging to the highest social caste in India.

Buddha: (*sangs-rgyas*) One who is totally purified from all defilements (*sangs*) and who has realized all that can be known (*rgyas*).

Calm abiding: (*zhi-gnas*, Skt: *shamatha*) A state of concentration in which the mind can abide one-pointedly and effortlessly on the object of meditation.

Chakra King: (*'Khor-lo bsgyur-pa'i rgyal-po*) A celestial being endowed with tremendous power and wealth.

Charvaka: (*rgyang-'phan pa*) A follower of a non-Buddhist materialistic philosophy current in ancient India. See note 55.

Chittamatrin: See note 36.

Conditioned existence: (*srid-pa*, Skt: *bhava*) Existence conditioned by disturbing conceptions and tainted actions; the same as cyclic existence.

Conqueror: (*rgyal-ba*, Skt: *jina*) An epithet for a Buddha, so called because he/she has overcome the four devils.

Cyclic existence: (*'khor-ba*, Skt: *samsara*) The continued experience of unsatisfactory states of existence resulting from actions produced by disturbing conceptions.

Dakini: (*mkha'-'gro-ma*) a form of being somewhat similar to a fairy or nymph. Some exist within cyclic existence, others are free from it.

Deceptive truth: (*kun-rdzob bden-pa*, Skt: *samvrtisatva*) This term refers to all existent phenomena other than emptiness, i.e. everything apprehended by the valid cognitions of ordinary beings. They are deceptive because the way in which they appear and the way in which they exist do not correspond: they appear as truly existent whereas in reality they are found to be empty of true existence.

Devil: (*'dud*, Skt: *mara*) There are four kinds of devils or demonic forces: death, disturbing conceptions, the aggregates of body and mind, and the evil celestial Devaputra.

Dharma: (*chos*) Generally religion, here the doctrine of Buddha.

Dharmakaya: (*chos-sku*) The fully realized and Awakened Mind of a Buddha.

Disturbing conceptions: (*nyon-mongs*, Skt: *klesha*) See note 7.

Emptiness: (*stong-pa nyid*, Skt: *shunyata*) The ultimate nature of all phenomena, their lack of true existence. See note 34.

Energy-winds: (*rlung*, Skt: *prana*) The light and mobile elements of the body, ranging from the gross breath to the many subtle currents of energy that, flowing through an intricate network of channels, allow for most physical functions to operate.

Hinayana: (*theg-dman*) The 'lesser spiritual pursuit' of the Shravaka and the Pratyekabuddha aimed at one's personal liberation alone.

Identitylessness: (*bdag-med*, Skt: *anatman*) In the Madhyamika system this refers to the emptiness of true existence of either the person (personal identitylessness) or other phenomena (phenomenal identitylessness).

Ishvara: (*dbang-phyug*) A divine being who, according to certain Hindu schools, is said to be the creator of the world and its inhabitants.

Karnapa: The name of a place in ancient India where competitions were held to see who could endure the most pain.

Kashyapa: (*'od-srungs*) An Arhat who was a personal disciple of Buddha Shakyamuni.

Ksitigarbha: (*sa'i snying-po*) lit: the 'heart of earth', the name of a Bodhisattva.

Madhyamika: (*dbu-ma-pa*) A follower of the Madhyamika philosophical school founded by Nagarjuna. See note 34.

Mahayana: (*theg-pa chen-po*) The 'great spiritual pursuit' of the Bodhisattva.

Manjughosha: (*'jam-dbyangs*) lit: 'the smooth melodious one', the name of the Bodhisattva of Wisdom.

Mayadevi: (*lha-mo sgyu-'phrul*) The mother of Buddha Shakyamuni.

Merit: (*bsod-nams*, Skt: *punya*) The wholesome forces and tendencies accumulated from virtuous actions of body, speech and mind.

Mighty One: (*thub-pa*, Skt: *muni*) An epithet for a Buddha, here specifically for Shakyamuni Buddha.

Nagarjuna: (*klu-sgrub*) A Buddhist sage who, with Asanga, helped to revive the Mahayana; noted for his elucidation of the Madhyamika philosophy of emptiness.

Naiyayika: (*rigs-pa can*) A follower of a Hindu school of philosophy. See note 52.

Nirvana: (*mya-ngan las 'das-pa*) The state of liberation from the sorrowful condition of cyclic existence. Sometimes this term is used as a synonym for emptiness. See note 39.

Other-cognition: (*gzhan-rig*) The aspect of mind that only has phenomena other than itself as its objects.

Padmapani: (*phyag-na pad-mo*) lit: 'the lotus holder', another name for Avalokiteshvara.

Pratyekabuddha: (*rang sangs-rgyas*) A follower of the Hinayana noted for living in isolation.

Primal substance: (*spyi gtso-bo*, Skt: *prakrti*) See note 21.

Realist: (*dngos smra-ba*, Skt: *bhutavadin*) See note 54.

Samantabhadra: (*kun-tu bzang po*) lit: 'the all good one', the name of a Bodhisattva.

Samkhya: (*grangs-can pa*) A follower of a Hindu school of philosophy. See note 50.

Sangha: (*dge-'dun*) lit: 'those who aspire for virtue', the realized beings who assist in one's spiritual development.

Self-cognition: (*rang-rig*, Skt: *svasamvedana*) The aspect of mind that only has itself as its object.

Shravaka: (*nyan-thos*) lit: 'a hearer', a follower of the Hinayana tradition noted for living in communities.

Special insight: (*lhag-mthong*, Skt: *vipasyana*) The heightened analytical faculty of mind that cognizes subtle impermanence and emptiness.

Sugata: (*bde-bar gshegs-pa*) lit: 'one who has gone to bliss', an epithet for a Buddha.

Sukhvati: (*bde-ba can*) The name of a Buddhist heaven or pure land.

Supushpachandra: (*me-tog zla-mdzes*) The name of a Bodhisattva whose deeds are recounted in the Samadhiraja Sutra. See note 31.

Sutra: (*mdo*) A discourse preached by a Buddha.

Tathagata: (*bde-bzhin gshegs-pa*) An epithet for the Buddha.

True existence: (*bden-par grub-pa*, Skt: *satya siddha*) The object to be negated in the investigation of emptiness. See note 34 and 37.

True perception: (*mngon-sum* Skt: *pratyaksa*) See note 38.

Ultimate truth: (*don-dam bden-pa*, Skt: *paramarthasatya*.) The true nature of all phenomena, i.e. their emptiness and identitylessness.

Vaibashika: (*bye-brag smra-ba*) A follower of a Hindu school of philosophy.

Vajradhvaja: (*rdo-rje rgyal-mtshan*) The name of a Bodhisattva mentioned in the Avatamsaka Sutra. See note 28.

Vajrapani: (*phyag-na rdo-rje*) lit: 'the holder of the vajra', the name of the Bodhisattva Power.

Valid cognition: (*tshad-ma*, Skt: *pramana*) An infallible state of consciousness that is able to induce certainty about its object. It can be either conceptual or non-conceptual.

Veda: (*rig-byed*) Ancient Indian hymns believed to have divine origin.

Yama: (*gshin-rje*) The Lord of Death.

Yogi: (*rnal-'byor pa*) A being who has developed calm abiding and special insight.

Bibliography

(The references for the entries marked 'P' are to the Peking edition of the Tibetan Tripitaka published by the Suzuki Research Foundation, Tokyo-Kyoto, 1956.)

C. Bendall and W.H.D. Rouse, trans. *The Shikshasamuccaya, A compendium of Buddhist Doctrine* (Motilal Banarsidass, Delhi, 1971).

Geshe Ngawang Dhargyey, *The Tibetan Tradition of Mental Development* (Library of Tibetan Works and Archives, Dharamsala, 1974).

M. Matics, trans. *Entering the Path of Enlightenment* (a translation of Shantideva's *Bodhicharyavatara*) (Macmillan, New York, 1970).

Geshe Rabten, *The Mind And Its Functions* (Tharpa Choeling, Switzerland, 1978).

Shantideva, *Bodhicharyavatara (byang chub sems dpa'i spyod pa la 'jug pa)* (P 5272, Vol. 99)

Shantideva, *Shikshasamuccayakarika (bslab pa kun las btus pa'i tshig le'ur byas pa)* (P 5336, Vol. 102)

Geshe Sopa and Jeffrey Hopkins, *Practice and Theory of Tibetan Buddhism* (Rider, London 1976).

Thog-me Zang-po (Thog med bzang po), *The Ocean of Good Explanation, A Commentary to (Shantideva's Guide to the Bodhisattva's Way of Life (byang chub sems dpa'i spyod pa la 'jug pa'i 'grel pa legs par bshad pa'i rgya mtsho)* (Sarnath, 1974).

Louis de la Vallee Poussin, trans. Introduction a la pratique des futurs Bouddhas (a translation of Shantideva's Bodhicharyavatara) (Librarie Bloud et Cie., Paris, 1907).